A New Wind Blowing!

Charles R. Tarr

D1562666

THE WARNER PRESS
ANDERSON, INDIANA

Printed in the United States of America

Contents

To
Betty my wife,
our four lovely daughters,
and the people of South Meridian and Anderson, Indiana,
whose honesty, openness, and love
enabled us to experience together
New Life in CHRIST

Foreword

When Moses saw the flaming bush in the desert, that it was not consumed, he moved aside to watch, then to listen to the voice of God.

In a sense, that is the way many feel today as revival fires are seen here and there around the world. God is getting our attention. While we cannot explain all the reasons for this new display of divine power, we know that something wonderful is happening.

One evidence of this awakening may be seen in Anderson, Indiana. Though but a small part of a much larger conflagration of God, it reflects in principle the spirit of revival in countless other places.

Reading the story is like opening a window in a stuffy room. There is a freshness and vibrancy in the author's witness. It throbs with the excitement of one who has stood out in the wind of the Spirit and felt the heavenly breeze blowing through his own life and ministry.

What God has done for one he will do for all who will let him. The form and method will vary with each person and church, but the touch of reality can be the same.

That is why I have such joy in commending to you this book. God's burning love for his children comes through. We are made to gaze upon his grace. And, if we would but listen, we may need to take the shoes off our feet.

—Robert E. Coleman

1

Is This Thing for Real?

"But about that time, a big blowup developed in Ephesus concerning the Christians."—Acts 19:23, LNT

On February 22, 1970, a spontaneous revival broke out in Anderson, Indiana, an industrial city of 75,000, and went unabated for fifty consecutive days. Within a few weeks, news of this spiritual awakening spread throughout the nation as witness teams fanned out into thirty-three states and even into Canada. The revival received nation-wide publicity as news releases hit the front page of the *Anderson Herald* and the *Indianapolis Star,* as well as featured articles in *The Chicago Tribune* and several national periodicals.

On that eventful day, a group of students from Asbury College came to the South Meridian Church of God to share what had taken place on that campus on February 3, 1970.[1] As these seven students shared what Christ had

---

[1] For a complete story, read *One Divine Moment,* (Fleming H. Revell Co., New Jersey) 1970.

done in their lives, the Holy Spirit descended upon this expectant and hungry people. Within minutes after they finished sharing, the altars were filled with people, young and old, seeking this fresh newness of life. (See Philippians 3:11, LNT.) And still they came—kneeling on the stairs leading to the pulpit and in the aisles! For more than two hours scores of Christians and non-Christians alike sought and found God. It was a modern outpouring of God's spirit in a manner that made it indisputable that "this is the Lord's doing, and it is marvelous in our eyes" (Ps. 118:23).

The services of this first day set the tone and pace for this spiritual awakening that continued fifty consecutive days, stretching from February 22 through April 12, with once-a-week services continuing until June. Untold thousands of lives were drastically changed as a result of this unusual visitation of the Holy Spirit.

The services were marked by their lack of formal structure and the confession and witnessing of laymen. One after another, different lay persons would walk to the pulpit and share their newfound faith. God used this method to speak to the hearts of many who would never have been touched by "formal" preaching. These testimonies varied according to the individual, but they were always marked by honesty and simplicity. Each one was asked to come to the platform to give his testimony and, even though the services were unstructured, they were never disorderly. On a given night the age groups might span at least three generations. Little children felt unashamed to share what Jesus meant to them; the aged would often be assisted in walking to the pulpit to share their experience; and the college youth sparked the meeting with their youthful exuberance.

Although the mood of the services seemed to vary from night to night, certain elements seemed to characterize each service. There was always a sense of hushed expectancy and reverence. Prayer and the reading of the Scriptures were vital to each service. There was such an awareness of the majesty of God that it always seemed appropriate for the congregation to kneel during prayer. The memory of observing a thousand worshipers fall to their knees and begin praying in low subdued tones (so they wouldn't distract those around them) will never be erased. Occasionally the congregation would pray for ten or fifteen minutes before someone would lead in corporate prayer. During these times one would often hear the quiet sobbing of someone praying for loved ones or for deep personal needs. Hundreds of prayer requests from all over the United States were sent to the church during this revival.[2]

There was always a sense of excitement in each meeting. In fact, the entire city of Anderson seemed to buzz with a new type of excitement as noonday meetings were held daily in City Hall. The impact was also felt in the public high schools as converted teen-agers quickly went to work to establish Campus Life organizations which drew crowds up to 400 within just a few days after their formation.[3] Anderson College was a beehive of spiritual activity as more than 750 students recorded decisions with their dorm mothers. One of the cheerleaders stood in church one night

---

[2]After two-and-one-half years we are still hearing of definite answers to many of the requests prayed over during 1970. Reports of the conversion of alcoholic fathers, the restoration of broken homes, and others still come to us.

[3]Within a few months a full-time director was secured to co-ordinate the efforts of Campus Life. It is still going strong.

to exclaim that she witnessed more excitement ("spirit" she called it) during the revival than at any athletic event of her college career. I actually saw people running to get into the church building forty-five minutes before the services were scheduled to begin!

An interesting sidelight was that the church building was always filled from the front to the back; a new precedent for this congregation!

As was to be expected, emotions ran high during the meetings, but it was a healthy, normal type of emotional expression. About the only visible demonstration of "emotionalism" occurred one night when an elderly man literally ran around the altar twice and then quietly sat down. A little boy told his mother about it, "Mommy, God got after a man last night and chased him around the altar twice but never did catch him!" A lovely black woman said in one of the meetings at the City Hall, "When you white folks get all worked up, something's bound to happen!"

This exuberance was also expressed through congregational singing. Songs such as "To God Be the Glory," "How Great Thou Art," " 'Tis So Sweet to Trust in Jesus," "Have Thine Own Way, Lord," "Just As I Am," and "There's a Sweet, Sweet Spirit in This Place" were sung practically every night. Each service was closed with the singing of "The Lord's Prayer," and each of us thrilled night after night in the singing of these great hymns.

As the decade of the sixties was characterized by the clenched fist, this revival was characterized by the raising of the hands and using E. Stanley Jones' slogan, "Jesus Is Lord!"

The meetings were also marked by an absence of any one leader. No mention was made of important personages who attended the meetings, although many of our national church leaders, musicians, and preachers attended these services. The one central personality was *Jesus Christ.*[4]

The meetings were also marked by the joy of the Spirit. One evening when a huge college football player came forward to accept Christ, he was practically tackled by his Christian buddies who had been praying for his conversion. It was impossible for a counselor to get to him and explain the plan of salvation, but after a little while he rose from the "mourners' bench" with the radiance of heaven on his face. He had the victory! A few weeks later I baptized this young man, and it was the first time that anyone requested prayer for me before he was baptized!

One evening a young college co-ed rose to her feet and asked the congregation to join her in "giving God a hand," and she began clapping her hands. Others soon joined in and within a few moments everyone found himself standing, applauding God. This was a new experience for all of us, and under normal circumstances may have appeared irreverent. But at that moment it was one of the most beautiful hymns I have ever heard as we gave our expression of praise to the God of the universe. It was beautiful!

The most powerful emotion of the entire meeting was *love*. The meeting was called "The Revival of Love." It was not a sentimental, "sticky" type of love; it was the pure love of God as described in First Corinthians 13. It was something one could "feel," and it drew people to Christ and to each other. Husbands and wives were reconciled, fathers and sons prayed together, the generation gap was bridged, and the racial barrier was lifted. The poem of Edward Markham described it in "Love Wins."

[4]Personal experiences and names are shared only to help others discover how to experience revival.

> *"He drew a circle that shut me out—*
> *Heretic, rebel, a thing to flout.*
> *But love and I had the wit to win:*
> *We drew a circle that took him in."*

This was the quality of the love we experienced during the revival—no one was outside or beyond the scope of God's love, regardless of age, culture, religion, or race.

The revival was also marked by its ethical and moral implications. Dr. James Earl Massey, Campus Minister at Anderson College, wrote, "The revival is a spiritual phenomenon of integrity. This happening has given to hundreds of students and adults an experience of genuine spiritual value. Counseling sessions with students have convinced me this happening has been deeper than mere emotion. . . . Scores . . . now have adopted proper standards for their lives. Christian beliefs have become important—and redemptive."[5]

The meeting was also characterized by a relaxed freedom in seeking God. No one seemed to be afraid of silence, those moments of deep heart-searching. Distressed persons wept unashamedly, and the unhurried atmosphere made it possible for them to seek God until they found him. For many this took time; time to leave the altar and be restored to a brother or sister. Time and again one would observe various persons resolving their differences and praying with each other. One person commented, "We all too often schedule a timeless God into a sixty-minute program. If he doesn't come then, he just doesn't come at all."

The Anderson Revival, 1970, bore many of the same marks as the Great Welsh revival of 1905. This revival

---

[5]James Earl Massey, *Vital Christianity,* April 19, 1970, p. 21.

began in Wales under the leadership of Evan Roberts and soon spread to the famous Charlotte Chapel in Edinburg. Joseph Kemp, pastor of the Charlotte Chapel, wrote the following about that awakening:

"It is impossible to convey any adequate idea of the prayer passion that characterized those meetings. There was little or no preaching, it being no uncommon experience for the pastor to go to the pulpit on the Lord's Day and find the congregation so caught in the spirit of prayer as to render preaching out of the question.

"The people poured out their hearts in importunate prayer. I have yet to witness a movement that has produced more permanent results in the lives of men, women, and children. There were irregularities, no doubt; some commotion, yes. There was that which shot itself through all prescribed forms and shattered all conventionality. But such a movement with all its irregularities is to be preferred far above the dull, dreary, monotonous decorum of many churches. Under these influences the crowds thronged the chapel, which only three years before maintained a 'sombre vacuum.' . . .

"There was nothing humanly speaking to account for what happened. Quite suddenly, upon one and another came an overwhelming sense of the reality and awfulness of His presence and of eternal things. Life, death, and eternity seemed suddenly laid bare. Prayer and weeping began, and gained in intensity every moment. As on the day of laying the foundation of the second temple, 'the people could not discern the noise of the shout of joy from the noise of the weeping of the people' (Ezra 3:13). . . .

"Then the prayer broke out again, waves and waves of prayer; and the midnight hour was reached. The hours had passed like minutes. It is useless being a spectator looking on, or praying for it, in order to catch its spirit and breath. It is necessary to be in it, praying in it, part of it, caught by the same power, swept by the same wind. . . .

"To the curious the meetings appear disorderly; but to those who are in them and of them, there is order in the midst of disorder. The confusion never gets confused; the meetings are held by invisible Hands. Believers have been awakened to a sense of having lived defeated lives, bound by the 'law of sin and death'; progress retarded by 'weights' and 'sins'; spiritual growth stunted by habits of various kinds. Over all these things victory has been claimed. Brethren have been reconciled to one another; differences which kept sisters apart have been destroyed."[6]

Naturally there were those who were skeptical of the revival, and Bob Quinn of *The Chicago Tribune* in commenting about this wrote, "Churchmen debate the significance of the marathon revival. Privately some ministers here have expressed doubts that the enthusiasm and faith generated during the meetings will last. But the event has been unique. The Reverend Mr. Tarr says it is the first such meeting of a major size that sprang up in a church facility in a community and not on a college campus. . . . Many people who came prepared to be skeptical at the emotional nature of the meetings have been impressed with the sincerity and the contagious atmosphere of the sessions. . . . In a day when many congregations are worried about losing their appeal to young people, 'Anderson's Revival of Love' seems to be saying something."[7]

---

[6]Stephen Olford, *Heart Cry for Revival,* (Fleming H. Revell Co. New Jersey, 1962) pp. 113-119.

[7]Bob Quinn, *The Chicago Tribune,* April 12, 1970, Section 1, p. 5.

The following note, handed to me during the revival, resolved a question asked by many people:

"The lady was from Southern California, the widow of a pioneer Church of God minister. When she heard rumbles about the revival in Anderson she wondered if it was the real thing. An idea came to her. She decided to call the information operator in Anderson. She felt that if this was real revival, the operator should have heard about it. After she got the operator on the line she commented, 'I hear that a revival is going on in Anderson. Do you know anything about it?'

"There was a pause on the other end of the line. Then the operator answered, 'Yes, there is a revival going on here. I attended the meeting last night and was saved!'

"These two talked for several minutes and the lady from California was convinced that this revival was for real!"

THINKING THINGS THROUGH

Let's Talk about It

1. How can one account for such a spiritual phenomenon as revival?

2. What causes many people to be skeptical of revival?

3. Is *revival* a word to the world or to the church? Why?

4. Is revival an activity of the church or an act of God? Explain the difference.

5. Who is responsible for revival?

Your Personal Quest

1. Reread this chapter slowly and carefully. Underline the elements of revival that you see as important and relevant to any authentic spiritual awakening.

2. How many of these elements are missing from your life?

2

But . . . Where Did It Begin?

**"Leave thy gift before the altar and go . . ."—Jesus,
Matthew 5:24**

It had been another sleepless night. For nearly three
years now I had not slept well, and tonight I felt unusually
discouraged and defeated. "Oh, well," I murmured, "If
I can't sleep I might as well get up for a while."

Going into the living room, I sat down on the couch and
began reflecting on the past. Thoughts both sweet and
bitter coursed through my mind.

Vividly I recalled an unusually meaningful experience
I had one night as I stood outside my home church in a
small town in eastern Kentucky. This little brick church
was particularly precious to me since it was here that I
had met Christ and had felt the call to the ministry. It was
a lovely summer night. The building was silhouetted
against the sky, and I wondered if I would ever have the
opportunity of pastoring a church as large and wonderful
as this. Just the thought of being called to preach made
goose pimples break out on my arms and I tingled with

excitement. That night I thought my heart was going to burst as I declared, "I'm going to be a preacher!" I was seventeen.

Four years later I was ordained into the ministry, and the years that followed were simply delightful. My young wife Betty and I were to pastor three congregations in Kentucky. Our first pastorate was a tiny little church in Petersville, Kentucky, and, although I had to drive forty-five miles one way to minister to this church, it was an unforgettable experience.

When I was twenty-one and Betty seventeen, we moved to Hope, Kentucky. There we spent five of the happiest years of our lives. However young and inexperienced we were, we dearly loved the church, and I learned one of the fundamental facts of the ministry—the congregation contributes as much to the life of the minister as the minister contributes to the life of the church. Betty and I just sort of "grew up" with this congregation. These were also the days when Betty and I struggled to get through college and learned what it meant truly to trust God.

Our next move was to Lexington, Kentucky, and the nine years we spent there had gone all too quickly. Actually this was one of those storybook pastorates. Things had gone so smoothly that it now seemed like one beautiful dream.

But these experiences were now only memories. Sweet, but still memories, and I knew that one could not forever live in the past. Two years before this eventful night, I had moved from Lexington to Anderson to one of the largest and finest congregations in our movement. I had every reason to be happy, excited, motivated, and fulfilled. But as I sat there alone in the dark, I was exceedingly unhappy; in fact I was miserable!

20

Suddenly it dawned on me that something dreadful had happened. I was no longer that young seventeen-year-old boy whose heart was pulsating with excitement and love. Instead, I was a frightened thirty-seven-year-old preacher. At that moment I was forced to look at the present and, more painfully, at myself.

Slowly I slipped down on my knees at the couch, yearning again for the romance of the Christian faith to return to my troubled heart. God really was speaking to me in these quiet reflective moments. Yet as I looked into my heart, I had to ask: Where is the eagerness to preach, the desire to win others for Christ? Where is the peace that has always assured me that he is near?

In my distressed and frightened mood I began seeking God. "Pray, that's it, Charles, pray!" So for possibly an hour I prayed earnestly and passionately for anyone and everyone that came to my mind. The result: nothing. Absolutely nothing! It seemed as if God had hidden his face from me and the heavens were made of steel. Then I stopped "praying." Cold sweat broke out on my forehead. All I could utter, and that almost under my breath, was: "Oh, God! Where are you? Why can't I find you? Please, God, please . . ."

Then there was silence.

Then it happened! "Charles, what are you going to do about David Turner?" At that moment God put his finger on the troubled spot in my life.

Dave had served as my associate during the latter part of my pastorate in Lexington. He had done a commendable job with the youth and the sanctuary choir. He was a wonderful young man, warm and friendly, but he and I were not able to relate meaningfully together. For some reason the chemistry wasn't right, and before I knew it,

21

it became next to impossible to communicate. Both of us were constantly on the defensive. After a year he submitted his resignation and returned to his home church—the congregation I was now pastoring!

The parting had not been pleasant and there was a wall a mile high between us. I had lived with this agonizing experience for nearly three years and it had been slowly destroying me. I developed stomach ulcers, insomnia, and a first-class case of "up tights." I lived almost constantly with a dull nagging headache.

The last year in Lexington found me nervous, insecure, and fearful. To illustrate how frustrated I was, one day as Betty and I left for our annual vacation, I again had one of my headaches. But just as soon as we got away from Lexington the headache eased and for two wonderful weeks I didn't think of a Bayer or Excedrin. However, as we were driving home from Florida the headache returned immediately when I saw the sign "Lexington"! Believe me, that's being "up tight."

I knew all along that this situation needed to be straightened out. I had made a few feeble attempts to apologize to Dave, but they all fell short. Even though the very mentioning of his name would make me panic inside, I covered quite well, and after a year or so I had pushed the whole incident deep into my unconscious mind. Actually I had done a pretty good job of forgetting it, and by the cunning of the human mind had rationalized that I actually didn't do anything that bad. Why not let bygones be bygones?

"Why don't you go to the phone and call him right now. Tell him you're sorry and ask his forgiveness?"

"Lord, don't you know it's two o'clock in the morning? Surely you're not suggesting that I call him now. One just doesn't call another person at two o'clock in the morning."

"Call him now!"

"Lord, I can't and I won't!"

"Yes, you can, and you will! That is, you will if you've been serious with me for the last hour or so."

Again there was troubled silence. Matthew 5:23-24 came to my mind and I simply couldn't get around it.

"If thou bring thy gift to the altar, and there rememberest that thy brother hath aught against thee; leave there thy gift before the altar, and go thy way; first be reconciled to thy brother, and then come and offer thy gift."

God had me and I knew it. For years I had preached that having a personal relationship with Christ was worth any price. But now a spiritual warfare was raging in my own soul, and little did I know of the far-reaching consequences in making the right decision. The battle continued for what seemed an eternity, although I suppose it was only thirty or forty minutes.

"Charlie Tarr, what in the world do you want at this ungodly hour?" laughed Dave Turner as he answered the phone sleepily.

This time I made no excuses, threw caution to the wind and blurted: "Dave, I have called to ask you to forgive me! I wronged you when we worked together in Lexington. I have been trying to rationalize about this for nearly three years. Dave, with my whole heart I seek your forgiveness."

After a brief pause Dave responded, "Charlie, you know I forgive you, and please forgive me too."

Dave was living in Beckley, West Virginia, at the time, and here at 2:30 A.M., while most of the citizens of Anderson, Indiana, and Beckley, West Virginia, were sleeping, two men wept, being reconciled. *Agape* flowed through those telephone lines that eventful night. This was one of

23

the most important single decisions I had made since my conversion experience.

One might wonder if the bells started ringing and the lights flashing, but it was not to be. I returned to the couch to pray but still felt rather empty and devoid of the Holy Spirit. But I had obeyed God. Tonight that was all that seemed really to matter.

Although I felt relieved that I had settled this particular problem in my life, this was only the beginning of a process that was to span several months and finally erupt in the greatest revival I had ever experienced. Whenever anyone asks me, "Charles, when did the revival begin with you?" I like to respond by saying, "It all began with a telephone call at 2:30 A.M.!"

THINKING THINGS THROUGH

Let's Talk about It

1. Is it true that revival usually precludes failure at one degree or another?

2. What is the place of obedience in revival. Discuss 1 Samuel 15:22.

3. Can one be out of fellowship with his fellowman and be in fellowship with God? Give some examples.

Your Personal Quest

1. Read the entire Sermon on the Mount—Matthew 5-7. Underscore any passages to which you feel you are not measuring up.

2. Sort out those areas that involve only you and *God* and those that involve you and *others*.

3

Take Off My Shoes?

Image had feet of clay—Daniel 2:33

As well as I can remember, the call to Dave was made in October of 1969. I told no one of it. It was nearly six months later that I discovered Betty had been strangely awakened as I had dialed his number and had walked quietly down the hall as she heard me talking to him. Not wanting to infringe on something so important to me, she said nothing about it.

For years I had often preached without a manuscript. Three or four weeks after the call, I was preaching one Sunday evening when I was strongly impressed to share the incident with my congregation. The very thought of doing this was shattering to my ego, but almost before I knew it I began relating what had happened. However, I was cautious not to mention any names. I took the cowardly route, saying "Once upon a time a friend and I had a little misunderstanding, *bla, bla, bla.*"

But God was not going to let me off that easily. Two weeks later, when I was again preaching, I was even more strongly impressed to relate the whole story, names and all! I could hardly believe what I was hearing myself say! Actually it was one of those rare experiences when it seemed as if it was not I who was speaking at all!

Here, before the whole congregation I had openly confessed that I had wronged a Christian brother. As I walked to the narthex I felt terribly stupid! That's right. Stupid! "What are they going to think of you now?" I muttered under my breath. But I had said it and I couldn't take it back. I would just have to live with the consequences.

God always knows what he is doing and it was certainly true in making this public confession. For the first time in nearly three years I could speak the name David Turner and not feel a knot in the pit of my stomach. I was relaxed and free!

In February, 1970, God completed the process of revival in my life. Early in that month the Division of General Service had planned a special consultation during which leaders from all over the nation had gathered to take an intensive look at the needs of our church. It was an historic event in the life of the church, but the most important part of the meeting for me happened on the sidelines.

I had always prided myself in not being prejudiced, but during that meeting I had to face another undeniable fact about myself—I didn't really love or feel concern for my black brothers. This hit me like a ton of bricks during one of the small group meetings when one of our outstanding black pastors, Benjamin Reid, shared some of the heartbreaking experiences he and some of his colleagues had suffered due to people like me. That night as I lay in my bed I saw how utterly self-centered I had been. I had never been refused admittance to a restaurant or service at a service station. I wondered how I would feel if I would have to take my family out into a field because we had been refused the use of restroom facilities. I shed hot, salty tears that night. Tears of concern for my black brothers and repentance for my own self-centeredness! I experienced love for the black race for the first time in my life. It was several months later that I read

"The opposite of love is not hate;
It is Apathy!"

Again I was called upon to seek reconciliation and forgiveness. During the last service of the consultation God spoke to me that I ought to go to Thomas W. Sawyer, currently Counselor to Black Students and Assistant Professor of Religious Studies, at Anderson College, and seek his reconciliation.

Thomas and I had served together on the World Service Division for four years, and at first had a wonderful fellowship. Then, slowly but surely, resentment began to build between us. It seemed that both of us had our axes to grind.

We were singing the last hymn during that service when I began to yearn to go to Tom and open my heart to him. Two hundred or more were assembled, and I had taken no special notice of who was sitting on the aisle across from me. Suddenly I glanced that way, and who was there but Thomas Sawyer!

Slowly I made my way to him as the last verse was being sung, and before it was completed I stood by his side and took his hand in mine. With tears in my eyes I said: "Tom, I want you to forgive me! I have felt resentment building between us and I'm sorry. Will you forgive me?"

Tom had tears in his eyes, too, and I will always treasure that moment when we embraced and experienced God's love flowing through us. I confessed to Tom that I wanted to love him and understand him. He responded in like manner. Having been born and raised in the hills of Kentucky, I knew little or nothing about the struggles one goes through in the huge metropolitan areas. We covenanted that day to listen (really listen) to each other and to love each other as *brothers!*

Three weeks later, February 22, 1970, revival came to our church and the final link in my own personal revival was put into place.

This fine congregation had been without a pastor for ten months before I accepted the call, and it had been a difficult time for them. Several ministers had candidated, but for some reason things just had not worked out for any of them to accept the pastorate. Finally they called me and, after the usual struggles any pastor goes through in making such decisions, I accepted.

Things had gone quite well and I was fairly well adjusted to Anderson and to the church. However a tormenting thought kept gnawing away at me, even though I said nothing about it to anyone. Although I would hardly admit harboring it in my heart, it was there like a thorn under my saddle!

During that eventful Sunday morning service I shared this hang-up with the church. "You have never given me the first reason to feel as I have for several months. You have treated me royally and a pastor could not ask for better cooperation and support. However, ever since I have been here I have been plagued by a silly, ridiculous thought. I know you candidated several pastors before I came, and I've been tormented by the thought that had you secured the pastor you really wanted it would have been someone other than I. What I felt you did was to scrape the bottom of the barrel and came up with me!"

Admittedly that was a crazy thing to say to a congregation and I don't recommend it to my colleagues. Yet as I said it, something very real and wonderful happened to me. It seemed as if the floodgates of heaven were opened between the congregation and me! I simply fell head over heels in love with this church in a depth that I had not known possible before!

I did not realize it, but my wife had some serious problems in loving the church too. Her problem came from a different direction, however. She had loved Lexington so deeply that it pained her grievously when we had to say good-by to such precious friends. "This time," she said, "I'm not going to get hurt when we have to leave." Therefore she determined to play the role of the perfect pastor's wife; except, she was not going to fall so deeply in love with the people. She played her role well

What both of us had done was to block the flow of love between the church and us. As a result Betty resented Anderson. She didn't like the stores ("I just can't find anything here in this town."). She couldn't stand the bumpy streets. She hated the weather. She with her crazy hang-ups and I with my silly hang-ups made quite a pair. Neither of us knew how the other felt. It is little wonder that so few victories were gained before 1970!

Betty's day of renewal was on its way, too! Two weeks after revival broke, Betty and I found ourselves standing before the church singing a special. We do not profess to be very good singers, but during the revival I believe God could have made a crow sound like a canary!

I sat down after we had sung, but Betty stayed at the pulpit. She always cries when she gives her testimony.

That morning she opened her heart as I had opened mine. Suddenly her well-laid plans went up in smoke (holy smoke!), and she experienced the same wonderful, indescribable love that had become mine two weeks earlier.

Betty now loved Anderson. Even the streets and railroad crossings didn't seem so bad. Now she was able to buy her dresses in "this" town, and the weather was, at least, tolerable!

Then it became clear why God impressed us to make our confessions:

He made us take off our shoes—not because the ground on which we were standing was holy—but to show us we had feet of clay!

It took me twenty-three years of living for the Lord before I learned this lesson. I needed desperately to learn it.

Why is it that we forget that even preachers are human? I had tormented myself for not always being right. In fact, from early childhood I couldn't stand to fail. I always had to be first in everything.

I suppose it is an admirable trait to want to succeed and not fail, but in my case these drives had become a two-headed monster. As a result even the slightest criticism put me in a spiritual tailspin, and, in an effort to protect myself, I tried to build a protective shell of "professionalism" around me. As a result I became a man all wrapped up in himself—and that is the smallest package in the world!

I learned that one could fail and yet still be loved by the Lord! I learned that far too many Christians are blocking God's love by foolish pride, resentment, and fear. When I learned this truth I became free! So much of the fear that formerly obsessed me is now gone, and I am a liberated person. As in the story of the Ancient Mariner,

The self-same moment I could pray;
And from my neck so free
The Albatross fell off, and sank
Like lead into the sea.

I'm convinced that confession is one of the most vital elements of Revival. "He that covereth his sin shall not prosper, but whoso confesseth and forsaketh them shall have mercy" (Prov. 28:13).

Confession opens the gates of love and closes the gates of fear. Besides, what is so bad in being at the bottom of the barrel anyway? The important thing is being in the barrel!

THINKING THINGS THROUGH

Let's Talk about It

1. Why is it helpful to make confession publicly? (James 5:16)

2. What cautions should be considered in making apologies, either public or private?

3. If one is really serious in setting his record straight, will God provide him with the proper opportunities to do so? Share your experiences.

Your Personal Quest

1. If you have difficulty in relating to someone, or if there has been alienation, go to that person in love and humility to ask his forgiveness. Do it soon!

2. Accept yourself and your humanity. Read 2 Corinthians 4:7-11.

4

"This Is Going to Cost Me $500.00!"

"He that covereth his sins shall not prosper."—Solomon, Proverbs 28:13

It had to be a difficult thing for a young man to say; especially before an audience of nearly a thousand. To make matters worse for him, the President of Anderson College was sitting on the front row taking in every word!

"This testimony is going to cost me $500.00! You see, I falsified one of my requests for a grant-in-aid at Anderson College. I want Dr. Reardon and the whole college to forgive me, and I'll do whatever is necessary to make it right!"

This testimony was typical of the ethical and moral elements that earmarked this unusual revival. Dr. Dale Oldham wrote the following article after attending several of the revival services:

"In all my 48 years in the ministry I have never seen anything like it. Last Sunday groups of students fanned out as far as Denver to witness to the Good News, and wherever they went the revival was born. Adults join young people in seeking forgiveness and new life in Christ. . . .

"As was to be expected, these meetings have their critics. The old familiar cry of 'emotionalism' is heard here and there, but strangely enough, most of the public services are in low key and subdued. There is no preaching and little special singing.

"Confession and witnessing are keynotes in this awakening. Both sins and faults are being confessed, and with confession comes forgiveness and healing. Witnessing to what the Lord has done follows, and the result is that others seek the Lord for their own needs.

"One wonders if this is not the Lord's way of bringing revival to the whole world—confession followed by earnest witnessing. It has worked at Asbury, Anderson, Azusa; perhaps it will work everywhere if we will follow the pattern and give God a chance."

Although instructions were never given as to how one should make restitution or confession, a pattern developed that illustrated how totally this movement was under the control of the Holy Spirit. Those sins that were committed privately were confessed only to God; against an individual, to that person; publicly, then to the group. The circle of confession was only as wide as the circle of commission. Never during the fifty days of revival was anything said publicly that caused embarrassment. This in itself was somewhat miraculous when one considers that the meetings continued for fifty days and, for the most part, consisted of testimonies and sharing of victories over past failures. Every great revival has been characterized by confession and repentance. Some of the things that were confessed were of a humorous nature after they were once out in the open.

One school teacher shared his most unusual testimony one night. He commented that he had become quite perturbed at a local member of the County Board of Education and decided to retaliate. He found a dead skunk and put it in the man's mailbox. When God began speaking to his heart, he knew he had to make that right.

Trembling, he went to the gentleman's home and, after passing the time of day, said, "Sir, do you remember finding a skunk in your mailbox last year?"

The man replied, "Yes, I do. And, I vowed if I ever found the culprit who did it I would shoot him!"

The teacher didn't know if he should go through with his idea or not about that time, but mustering up all the courage he could find, he blurted out, "Well, I'm that man! I've professed being a Christian for many years, and, in fact, I now teach a Sunday school class, but just within the past few days, I have been attending a revival. God has spoken to my heart pointing out how terrible my act against you really was. Please forgive me!"

The man hesitated for a few moments and then replied, "Well, I've still got half a mind to shoot you, but since you have been so nice to come and tell me, I'll forgive you."

The deepest work wrought in the hearts of thousands of persons, however, was simply between them and God. Another important event in my own personal process of revival occurred while I was attending a Life Institute in Arrowhead Springs in San Bernardino, California. It was a refreshing experience to visit California at that time of the year since it was bitter cold in Anderson during that particular January.

During one of the training lectures, Dr. Bill Bright, President and Founder of Campus Crusade, brought to our attention that the word *confession* carries with it the meaning of "saying along with God." I had never quite thought of it that way, but it really made sense to me. If God says that something in one's life displeases him, instead of rationalizing about it he should simply agree with God—"Say along with God"—and accept his forgiveness.

Dr. Bright instructed each of us to get alone with God and write down on a sheet of paper every impression we might have concerning things that might displease God. When I first heard him say that I thought surely there wouldn't be very many things on my list!

Within a few moments, though, I found myself out under the beautiful California skies, totally alone with God and with my thoughts. I began writing down the things that God seemed to say displeased him, and I was surprised at the long list. Although I wasn't pleased with the long list I had written, I discovered that instead of arguing with God and rationalizing about those things that displeased him, when I confessed them to God, I experienced forgiveness and an inner spiritual catharsis.

I'll never forget standing over a trash barrel moments later, tearing up this list, and claiming the promise of John 1:9, "If we confess our sins, he is faithful and just to forgive us our sins, and to cleanse us from all unrighteousness." It was most refreshing to be completely honest and open to God, and to myself.

Time and time again confession has been the key that has unlocked the storehouse of God's grace for thousands of Christians. I have tried to illustrate it by the diagram on the next page.

Whenever one is converted the love of God fills his heart. "And hope maketh not ashamed; because the love of God is shed abroad in our hearts by the Holy Ghost which is given unto us" (Rom. 5:5). The natural, or

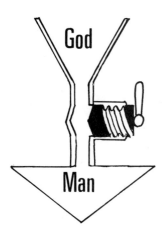

unsaved, man cannot make himself love God. As one confesses his sins and receives Christ as his personal Savior and Lord, God's love comes pouring in. Faith in Christ opens the valve between God and man. "For God took the sinless Christ and poured into him our sins. Then in exchange, He poured God's goodness into us!" (2 Cor. 5:21, LNT).

I'm sure that God's ideal is for his love constantly to fill our hearts and lives. However, human experience has taught us that very few Christians continuously keep this valve open between them and God. Even little things can shut us off from the things of God. One does not trip over wall-to-wall carpet; it is those throw rugs that our wives so lovingly place at strategic places over the house that break our arms!

When one disobeys God, the valve closes:

37

This is why we need revival! "Revival should be a constant reality. The idea that it is 'a thing of special times and seasons' owes its inception to the inconsistent nature of man and not of the will of God. Unfortunately, for most of us, despite our professions there comes those periods of spiritual sluggishness which make revival necessary. But if we lived in the continual fullness of the spirit of Christ, as God desires, revival would be an abiding state of experience."[1]

Most of the things we need to confess to God have sort of crept up on us. James tells us of the regressive nature of falling from grace: "Every man is tempted, when he is drawn away of his own lust, and enticed. Then when lust hath conceived, it bringeth forth sin: and sin, when it is finished bringeth forth death" (Ja. 1:14-15).

---

[1]Robert Coleman, *Dry Bones Can Live Again,* (New Jersey, Fleming H. Revell Co.) 1969, p. 14.

Many of those things that necessitate the need for revival come through that slow, deadly process. However, it doesn't take scandalous sins to separate one from God. Such things as resentment, ill will or jealousy have the same result—spiritual death or separation:

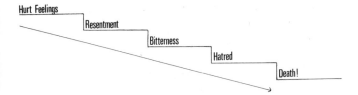

Perhaps Dr. Oldham is right; confession may be the Lord's way of bringing revival to the whole world. I know by experience that when one confesses, "says along with God," and trusts completely in Christ, the valve opens and he gets "in the flow." "If any man thirst, let him come unto me, and drink. He that believeth on me, as the scripture hath said, out of his belly shall flow rivers of living water. But this spake he of the Spirit, which they that believe on him should receive: for the Holy Ghost was not yet given; because that Jesus was not yet glorified" (John 7:37-39).

(See page 40.)

THINKING THINGS THROUGH

Let's Talk about It

1. Discuss the meaning of "the circle of confession being only as wide as the circle of commission." Does this make sense to you?

2. Does the concept of "living in the flow" have personal meaning to you?

Your Personal Quest

1. Get a pencil and a sheet of paper and get alone with God. Ask him to tell you what displeases him. List these things, large and small, as they come to your mind. Don't hurry this process. Don't argue with God. After you have "said along with God," take step two:

2. Write the Scripture reference 1 John 1:9 in bold letters on this list and destroy it. Claim the dual promises of forgiveness and cleansing.

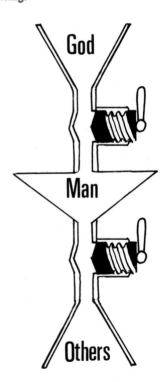

5

These . . . Firebrands?

**The Lord . . . maketh his ministers a flaming fire.
—David, Psalm 104:4**

The week prior to the revival the Lord taught me a truth
that has drastically altered my ministry. It all began when
a lovely, elderly woman called me one Saturday afternoon
to ask if I had heard of an unusual revival that had broken
out at Asbury College. She briefly told me about what had
taken place on the campus of my Alma Mater and concluded by asking if I would consider having a team visit
our church to share what was happening. I told her I
would make it a matter of prayer. After a few hours I was
strongly impressed that I should call Asbury College and
check it out.

The memory of that call is very clear. I sat down and
listed three persons at Asbury whom I knew quite inti-
mately. The first two were professors, one at the college
and the other at the Seminary, and the third person was
a young seminarian who had served as my associate for a
short time a few years earlier. Before dialing the operator,
I listed them in the order I would call them. However,
when the operator answered the dial, I asked for the name

of the person who was last on the list I had just made. It was an impulse, but I suddenly knew that the person to contact was the young seminarian, Jimmy Usher.

I had no way of knowing that Jimmy had been burdened for Anderson College for several days. For some reason he had not been able to make the proper contacts with persons who were interested in having a team come to the Anderson campus. Just prior to my calling him he had been thinking of Anderson and praying that a door would be opened for him and a group of students to share the unusual story of how God had poured out his Spirit on that small Kentucky college. God had planned this moment and it was *beautiful*. Jimmy had scheduled several Sundays in advance, but the Sunday I wanted him to come was open —February 22, 1970! He responded excitedly and said he would get a team and arrive in Anderson late Saturday afternoon on February 21.

It is not difficult to have a large attendance in Anderson when one plans something special and advertises it sufficiently. On Thursday morning (the 20th) the idea of advertising this special service hit me and I decided to call the *Anderson Herald* and put in a $50.00 ad. I was quite sure that by doing this we would have a large turnout for both services. I was suddenly, almost abruptly, checked by the Holy Spirit from doing this. "If this is real revival, why don't you let God do it his way, and if this is really a movement of the Holy Spirit don't dare exploit it. Don't try to *make* things happen, *let* them happen!" This was the lesson that was to have life-changing implications for me.

So instead of putting in a $50.00 ad that I now feared might be exploiting something sacred, I simply asked my secretary to type the announcement of our Sunday service and put it in the space the newspaper provides without charge for all the local pastors to list their sermon topics for Sunday morning and evening services.

Later that week, Friday as well as I can recall, I received a call rather late in the evening. A woman introduced herself as Miss Viola Phillips, the Religious News Editor for the *Anderson Herald*. She inquired about the announcement that had been turned in regarding our Sunday services. "Reverend Tarr," she said, "I've been reading about this revival at Asbury and I'm very interested in it. I see you are having a group of Asbury students with you this Sunday. I wondered if you would mind if I did an editorial on it for the Saturday paper?" I almost fell off my chair! In my heart I said, God I knew you worked quickly—but I didn't know you worked this quickly!

I tried to subdue my excitement long enough to assure Miss Phillips that we would be honored to have her write the editorial about our Sunday services.

At that moment I made a private covenant with God that should revival break out, I would never ask for opportunities of sharing or propagating it. If doors were to be opened, God would have to open them—not I. I would not try to make things happen. I would let them happen. For too long I laid my plans and then saw to it that they were carefully executed. The trouble was that usually very little or nothing happened.

No amount of money could have purchased this prime space in our local newspaper:

Asbury Delegation to Tell Local Church of Dynamic Campus Revival

"An extraordinary revival upsurge this month has swept the campus of Asbury College, Alma Mater of E. Stanley

Jones, and other campuses in 19 states have now felt the impact through the witness of Asbury students and faculty. Asbury classes were dismissed a week for the thrust of "confession, repentance, and revival" and on February 8 several community churches dismissed their services to unite in the revival. This Sunday a group from Asbury College will relate the experience which originated and has continued and spread not through preaching, but by confession, witness, and prayer."

By now I was beginning to sense how powerfully God was working, but this was only the beginning. When I saw the group of seven students who came to the parsonage on Saturday afternoon, the first impression was, What can these students possibly do for us? I soon discovered that of the students, most of them were underclassmen in college and only one was a seminarian! Actually they didn't look like "firebrands" to me, but the thoughts of how things were fitting together prevented me from harboring negative thoughts about them.

Later that Saturday evening we all became convinced that something wonderful was about to happen. During our evening prayer time with the students and my family, I shared a scripture God had laid on my heart a few weeks earlier and, although I couldn't quite see its connection to our church situation, I felt it was, somehow, important. I read it aloud, "My (God's) power shows up best in weak people" (2 Cor. 12:9b, LNT).

All of a sudden, one of the young co-eds let out a squeal. "Oh," she said, "I was praying this morning asking God to give me a verse that would assure me that he could use me during these services. You see, I've never been on one of these witnessing teams and I'm scared to death. When I opened my Bible, my eyes fell upon 2 Corinthians

12:9 and I claimed it for my very own! I told God how weak I was and he seemed to say, 'Good, that's the type of person I'm looking for! My power shows up best in weak people!' "

All of us rejoiced in this unusual experience. We received confidence from God's Word that he would use this group of humble Spirit-filled students to ignite the fires of revival in our church.

When I retired that Saturday evening, I lay awake for awhile thinking about Sunday's service. God gave me an unusual thought to share at the very beginning of the service, and I felt such a surge of excitement that I could hardly find sleep.

Excitement continued to run high the next morning as we awaited the service. Those involved in leading our worship services always met in a small hallway underneath the pulpit area to pray and seek God's guidance. As the eight of us joined hands to form a circle of prayer, we sensed the presence of God so strongly that we could hardly pray! We did not realize it, but revival was headed our way like a steamroller! We all walked to the platform, knelt briefly in prayer, and then God moved in!

"Ladies and gentlemen, I need your help this morning. Last night a very special and dear friend of mine promised me that he would be in our service today, but I can't seem to spot him in the audience. He may be in the balcony, or in the back of the church, or perhaps near the front—but I just can't find him. He may be sitting next to you or in front of you. Would you mind checking this out for me? Oh, his name? His name is *Jesus!*"

What a day February 22, 1970, was! The service was marked with simplicity, honesty, and freedom. These students became instruments in the hand of God to ignite

45

the fires of revival in Anderson. Intentionally we disbanded the use of a bulletin on this particular Sunday since we wanted it to be an unstructured service. One by one each student would walk to the pulpit and share out of his heart what Christ had done in his life. One of the young women told how she had been a chronic liar and was unable to tell the truth about anything. But after she confessed this sin to God, he forgave and cleansed her of this bondage.

Another young woman was a Spanish-American, and she sang one of the most beautiful songs one would ever want to hear. The Holy Spirit so anointed her voice that her song broke the hearts of those who listened. The title of the song was, "Without Him I Could Do Nothing." She would sing one verse in English and another in Spanish. Although I don't understand Spanish, when she sang the chorus, I was thrilled beyond words.

> *Cristo, O Cristo, lo conoces tu hoy?*
> *no rehaces al Rey-*
> *O Cristo, O Cristo,*
> *sin Cristo, yo no soy nada.*

Then the service broke open! Scores of persons, Christian and non-Christian alike, broke loose for the altar until there was no room to kneel. They kept on coming until people were kneeling in the aisles and at their pews seeking God.

One person who was destined to play an extremely important role in the continuation of the revival, Professor Sid Guillen, sensed a great need in his life, and he simply had to get to the altar to pray. Like Zacchaeus, he couldn't get there for the crowd. He was sitting on the front row with a screen between him and the altar. Since he could not get there any other way, he jumped over the screen and made a life-changing decision for Christ!

This altar service lasted until 2:00 P.M. and we finally dismissed the service at 2:30 P.M.! As far as I know not one person left the church, although many roasts and hams were burning in the ovens at home. But this was more important than physical food—this was manna from heaven!

No one had to urge the congregation to return for the 6:00 o'clock Sunday evening service. This service lasted until 10:00 P.M., and it was even greater, much greater, than the Sunday morning service. There was no formal preaching, just singing and sharing and weeping and rejoicing. True revival had come, and even now as I attempt to describe it all words fail.

During the service I asked Jimmy Usher if he and some of the students could stay over for Monday night. I had never witnessed anything like this during my twenty years in the personal and evangelistic ministry, and it was totally out of the picture to close the meeting. Since Jimmy said he could stay over, we announced that we would have another service on Monday evening at 7:00 P.M.

We had 510 in the service Sunday morning and 505 Sunday evening. When we returned to the church at about 6:00 P.M. on Monday evening the church was already nearly filled! By 6:30 you could hardly get in the sanctuary. At 7:00 people were standing around the walls of the sanctuary, out in the narthex, and in every conceivable place one could find. More than a thousand attended this service. If the two services on Sunday were Great (with a capital "G") this service was simply too much for words! Even after two-and-one-half years I still get the "tingles" when I think of the awesome power of God that fell on that service.

This meeting belonged to no one but God! His power was showing up magnificently in *weak* people, as students and laymen would simply share with the congregation what Jesus Christ had done for them. After a testimony the altars were flooded again and again. There was no way to determine how many were saved, healed, or filled with the Holy Spirit during those three services. It was impossible to counsel with those who came forward—one simply couldn't get to them. But God was there, and it was *he* whom these persons were seeking. Some sat on the edge of their seats—others stood—but everyone seemed to bathe in the presence of God for nearly four wonderful indescribable hours! This had to be one of the greatest nights of my life. Here, without advertising, without a lot of fanfare, with no planning, pleading, or begging, we *saw God work!*

THINKING THINGS THROUGH

Let's Talk about It

1. What are we doing in our church that we could not do if the Holy Spirit would withdraw from us?

2. What is the difference between "making things happen" and "letting them happen"?

3. If things aren't happening in our church, where is the trouble?

4. What qualifications must one have to be used of God?

Your Personal Quest

1. Accept the *fact* that God wants to use *you!* Open yourself to him. Allow his love to flow through you to someone else today.

2. Don't struggle to witness. Listen and be sensitive to the Spirit's leadership. Let God's power work through you.

48

6

Give It Away?

"He that loseth his life . . . shall find it."—Jesus, Matthew 10:39

This was New Testament revival in the twentieth century! For years I had longed to witness and be a part of such a spiritual awakening, but now that God had moved in upon us in such awesome power, it almost seemed unreal.

On Monday, February 23, I went along with the witness team to the campus of Anderson College to mingle with the students and to share with them what was happening. We had several opportunities to witness and we were aware that God was working. One of those unforgettable experiences took place that beautiful wintry afternoon in a little valley at the south side of the Seminary building. Several persons had gathered there and were talking about the revival when someone suggested that we pray. The small group joined hands and as we prayed we sensed the gentle breeze of God fanning our souls. Nothing emotional. Just Presence. This was before the Monday night crowd of nearly one thousand. When we walked to the platform and saw the crowd, we were all overwhelmed. That night we witnessed an altar service that lasted two hours.

I suppose that was the reason I was totally unprepared for the mood of depression and discouragement that settled upon me after we returned home and finally retired around 1:30 A.M. I felt utterly incapable of giving guidance to such a mammoth, spontaneous movement of the Holy Spirit. I couldn't understand why God had chosen a local church four or five miles from the college campus to spearhead this revival. For the most part this revival movement had occurred on college campuses, and we had heard that Anderson College was the twenty-first college to experience this spiritual awakening. I felt a great love and concern for the many students at Anderson College, but I recognized that my main responsibility was for the local congregation. I knew this was too big for me. I was confused and didn't know what should be done in continuing this meeting.

After whispering these concerns to God, I fell into a deep restful sleep. At exactly 6:20 A.M. I was suddenly awakened as if someone had touched my arm very lightly; the way a mother awakens a child. The frustration and depression of a few hours previous were gone and a deep sense of peace and tranquillity now flooded my heart. I knew what God wanted me to do.

Reaching for the phone, I called five or six local pastors and laymen who were at the meeting on Monday evening and asked them if they could meet me at Don's Restaurant at 7:30 A.M. for breakfast. There was something I wanted to share with them.

Two of the laymen I had felt impressed to call were strangers to me. When I first saw them in the service on

50

Monday evening, I actually thought they opposed the meeting. However, a couple of hours later I met these men in the balcony of the church (the service was still going on) and they walked up and introduced themselves. They shared how they had been praying for a revival like this for many years. These two fine laymen said they would be glad to meet with us.

I was trusting God for eight to ten persons with whom I could share my concern. When I arrived at Don's, 20 men were there! One could sense their excitement. My proposal was simple: I wanted to give the revival away. I shared with the men that I felt this revival was larger than one church, or one man, or one denomination or movement. I could foresee this being a city-wide meeting where Christians of all faiths could share in God's glory! My plan was simple: I requested that we move to another location—a neutral place—where all Christians regardless of church affiliation would feel free to participate. "Gentlemen," I said, "I want to give this revival away—to you!"

Their response startled me. "No, Brother Tarr, we don't feel that would be the right thing to do. The Holy Spirit has fallen on the church and the building itself seems to be sensitized to his presence. It would be a mistake to make this change."

One of the men added, "Why can't we have a noonday meeting at City Hall? Is that neutral enough?" I remarked that it sounded great to me. Before I could enumerate how difficult, if not impossible, it might be to secure that facility, the gentleman added, "I know the mayor. If you don't object, I'll make the arrangements!"

Within less than an hour, God had opened doors I never even dreamed of. The Council Chambers of the new City Hall were secured for the weekdays from 12:00 noon to

1:00 P.M., and the Christian Business Men's Fellowship had volunteered to take complete charge of the meetings.

The very next day these noonday services began in City Hall and they continued until the revival ended—some 46 days later!

The following news release appeared in the *Anderson Herald* on Thursday, February 26, 1970.

Asbury Revival Enters City Hall

"The Asbury Revival spirit, which has drawn more than a thousand persons nightly to South Meridian Church of God yesterday noon invaded the City Council Chambers in the new City Building.

"About 250 business and professional persons, ministers and high school students crowded into the Council Chambers for prayer and other expressions of concern and faith."

These Spirit-sensitive men were correct regarding our keeping the night services in the church. Without announcement, all day long people came and went into the church to pray. Many were converted within minutes after walking into the sanctuary. Others would begin weeping, seeking God. It reminded me of 2 Chronicles 7:1-3: "Now when Solomon had made an end of praying, the fire came down from heaven, and consumed the burnt offering and the sacrifices; and the glory of the Lord filled the house. And the priests could not enter into the house of the Lord, because the glory of the Lord had filled the Lord's house. And when all the children of Israel saw how the fire came down, and the glory of the Lord upon the house, they bowed themselves with their faces to the ground upon the pavement, and worshipped and praised the Lord saying, 'For He is good; for his mercy endureth forever.'"

Meeting with this group also was the beginning of the most unusual fellowship I have ever known. Some of the more frequently asked questions concerning the meeting are: How was it directed? Surely the meeting didn't continue for fifty days without someone taking charge? This observation is correct.

From this group of twenty men, a smaller group was formed which gave direction to the meeting. We did not form any committees or vote on issues. We simply were drawn together irresistibly by the Holy Spirit. This was one of the most God-directed groups I have ever been associated with. They simply surrounded the whole meeting with their loving concern. In 1 Samuel 10:26 we read, "There went with him a band of men, whose hearts God had touched."

What drew us together had to be the Holy Spirit. Of the ten men who formed this "inner circle," I only knew four of them before February 22. We never discussed the possibility of doctrinal differences, even though several different church groups were represented in this group. The theme, "Jesus is Lord," gave impetus to the task of making him known in our community.

To a man, each one had experienced personal revival! Most of them had experiences that would justifiably merit more testimony than I have space to mention here. These men, immediately upon being revived, saw the need to evangelize Anderson with the gospel. The "inward look" soon changed to the "outward look"—seeing the many needs of our city.

Each found his place in giving direction and meaning to what was happening such as—

* One gave guidance in counseling the new converts.

53

* Another felt the burden to organize the witness teams that were scattering all over the nation.

*One assisted on the platform.

* Another small group would be in prayer *during* the service. Often when it seemed as if Satan was fighting the meeting, these men would leave the service and go to a small room they had selected as a prayer room. Oh, how they would wrestle with God, and invariably, soon after they began praying the meeting would again break loose!

* Others were burdened for propagating the meeting. We left this aspect completely to them, and what a job they did!

* Others took care of the physical details—such as preparing the school gymnasium for our Sunday afternoon rallies.

Everything was done in complete unity. It was almost frightening how the Lord led us in every decision. It seemed as if every member of the group would be impressed at the same time in the making of important decisions. Events as recorded in Acts 15:28, "It seemed good to the Holy Ghost and to us" became meaningful to us experientially.

Without doubt it was the deep spiritual guidance of this group that protected the meeting from the excesses and confusion that often exploit such spiritual outpourings. The fact that those men were from different churches helped tremendously in allowing the meeting to be ecumenical. For the first time in my ministry I saw people of all faiths join together under the banner "Jesus Is Lord!" This was the most authentic expression of the New Testament church I have ever seen.

Dr. Thomas Carruth of Asbury College Seminary said in one of the Sunday afternoon services, "When you folk and the followers of John the Baptist, and John the Wesley get together, something has to happen!" Of course, this is what it takes if we are going to experience nation-wide revival: We must quit splitting hairs over doctrinal issues. We must rid ourselves of the bigotry and prejudice that keeps Christian brothers and sisters separated. How small and insignificant our differences seem when we open ourselves to God's love. We live in the flow—and if revival is valid—it always includes the dimension of caring for others.

If the valve is closed between man and his fellowman, he cannot experience the exhilarating joy of continual revival.

Those conditions that bring revival focus on our personal inner needs:

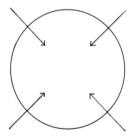

But once we move into that vital relationship of knowing Christ personally and experiencing the infilling of the Holy Spirit, the attention then goes outward.

55

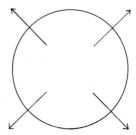

And God ministers through us! Think of it! God is love, power, wisdom, peace—all that any man could ever need. But only as we *give him away* do we "live in the flow."

This is the reason that many of our programs and efforts are so futile and barren! We think only of ourselves—our church, our attendance, our reputation. As a result we *cut* ourselves off from God!

"Look not every man on his own things, but every man on the things of others. Let this mind be in you, which was also in Christ Jesus: Who, being in the form of God, thought it not robbery to be equal with God: But made himself of no reputation, and took upon him the form of a servant, and was made in the likeness of men: And being found in fashion as a man, he humbled himself, and became obedient unto death, even the death of the cross. Wherefore God also hath highly exalted him, and given him a name which is above every name."—Philippians 2:4-9

This may shock you. Our congregation in some ways suffered because of the revival. Why? Because we attempted to "give ourselves away in mission!" On some Sundays several hundred students and members of the church were out in other churches sharing what Christ had done for them. I announced on one occasion that it would please me if I came to church one Sunday morning and found no one there, providing, of course, they would be scattered all over the United States sharing the Good News! We experienced the completeness of the joy of the Spirit as we gave ourselves in selfless love (John 15:11).

The secret is—as we lose ourselves, we find ourselves! The more we attempt to "Give Christ Away," the more we have of him! The Christian or the church that is concerned only about self-preservation will *die!* Those who give themselves away receive and live.

Sometimes it takes a long time to see the abiding fruit of this type of selfless love. On April 13, 1970, (fifty-one days after the revival began I received a call from one of the men I called on that eventful Tuesday morning, February 24. He asked if I could have dinner with him and his business associate. His associate was not saved and he was deeply burdened for him. I wanted to stay home badly that night as I was utterly exhausted. Naturally, Betty also wanted us to have an evening at home with the girls, but she knew I should go and encouraged me to do so. Later that night, at 11:55 P.M., this businessman was converted.

Nearly a year later I was in a staff meeting at the Board of Church Extension when some of our men were discussing an exciting event that had just happened at a church where they conducted a Fund Campaign. They commented that a man in Illinois had given a tract of land valued at $50,000.00 to our church on which to erect this new building. I asked, "What was his name?" It was the man who was saved at 11:55 P.M. in a downtown office building in Anderson, Indiana!

THINKING THINGS THROUGH

Let's Talk about It

1. In general are we more concerned about ourselves—our own self-preservation—than we are about others? Give illustrations.

2. How can Christians work effectively together without agreeing at every theological point?

3. What is the difference between building a local church and building the Kingdom?

Your Personal Quest

1. Begin praying for God to place you in a small group of Christians. Perhaps you could form such a group in your congregation.

2. Surround your pastor and congregation with your loving concern and prayer. This could become a real ministry for you.

7

Is This Really Happening to Me?

"I was in the Spirit."—John the Revelator, Revelation 1:10

It is strange what happens to a person when he disobeys God even at a small point in his life. Compared to many church situations with which I have been acquainted, what transpired in my life before the revival was quite insignificant. However, the effects of even a small act of disobedience are sometimes devastating.

Not too many months ago I was flying into Washington, D.C., when the captain of the 727 came on the intercom and said, "Ladies and gentlemen, we are approaching our nation's capitol. If it were not for the mist you could see many historic landmarks clearly." A thin mist in the atmosphere distorted our view of the Pentagon, the Washington Monument, the Capitol Building, and other famous buildings.

So it is in our relationship with God. One does not have to commit adultery or get in a fist fight in a Board of Trustees meeting to lose his relationship with God. For example, when Peter was giving instructions to husbands, he commented, "Likewise, ye husbands, dwell with them according to knowledge, giving honor unto the weaker vessel, as being heirs together in the grace of life; that your prayers be not hindered" (1 Pet. 3:7).

Did you ever try to pray after having an argument with your spouse? These prayers don't go very far, do they? The argument creates a mist that prevents our seeing clearly the things of the Spirit. One man inquired, "Let me ask the $64,000 question. Has the revival made any difference in your homelife?" Authentic revival will always make an impact on the home, for we wear no masks at home and the first persons who will realize that we are changed will be the members of our family. Personally, the very walls of our home seemed saturated with the presence of God during the revival, and the depth of understanding and love that invaded our home still lingers.

Couples, young and old, exclaimed that God put new love in their marriage. When the goal of both mates becomes Christ instead of two individual, selfish pursuits; then that couple really becomes one in Christ. It is surprising how meaningful life can become and how smoothly God can resolve our problems when Christ is on the throne. But if self is on the throne and each partner seeks his own way, trouble is inevitable. Christ is the friend of every marriage and seeks to be a vital member of each family. I feel sorry for the husband and wife who go their separate ways, never discovering the joy of working together in pursuing the highest goal in life—that of fulfilling Christ's will. Let me illustrate:

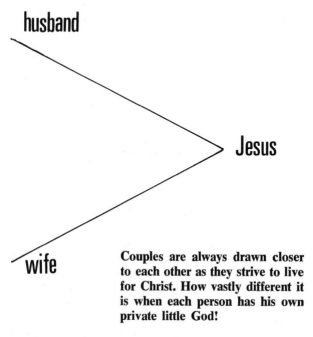

Couples are always drawn closer to each other as they strive to live for Christ. How vastly different it is when each person has his own private little God!

One of the most unusual conversions of the entire revival centered around a problem home. A marriage was in danger of dissolving, and a third party was involved. The wife was a lovely Christian who held on to God for her husband's return to Christ. Not only was he saved, but the wife helped lead her husband's former girl friend to Jesus Christ. This is revival!

It was no wonder that a few months later while I was preaching one Sunday this attractive, quiet, unassuming woman who loved God so deeply held up a flash card about two-thirds of the way through my sermon. It read:

Praise the Lord!

Then in a few moments she held up another one:

Hallelujah!

Can you imagine what this would do for a preacher from the hills of Kentucky?

Toward the latter part of the revival another fine young woman came to the altar. As I knelt across from her, I inquired if I might assist her in any way. "Oh, Brother Tarr," she sobbed, "I have a violent temper that I can't control, and I simply must gain victory over it!"

I could hardly believe what I heard. I knew Doris quite well, I thought, and I always viewed her as being rather docile, quiet, and easygoing. About that time she looked up and pounded the altar rail with her fist and said, "I'm so impatient! When I want something done, I want it done *now!* And when it isn't done, I get angry. Well, worse than angry, I get downright mad." After we had prayed, Doris went to the pulpit and shared her newfound victory with the congregation. Evidently many others had similar needs since the altars were quickly lined with people seeking help from God.

Something far more significant occurred as a result of Doris' obedience other than the response it kindled in her.

Doris' husband and father-in-law were both unsaved, and for several years the church had faithfully prayed for their salvation. Both of these men lived exemplary moral lives. In fact, they attended church every Sunday morning, Sunday evening, and many times on Wednesday evenings. They tithed to the church, had no bad habits, but neither of them would accept Christ.

I do not think it inconsequential that four nights later Larry, Doris' husband, and Lester, her father-in-law, both came forward and were gloriously saved. What a thrill it was to baptize four members of that one family a few nights later! Doris could have rationalized by saying, "Everyone has a temper, and so what if my fuse is a little short?" However, her impatience and temper created just enough mist that she could not see the heavenly landmarks clearly. After she confessed her need to Christ and received the Holy Spirit, the mist lifted.

But what happens when one disobeys God and doesn't confess it and make proper restitution? As I said at the beginning, the result is that one begins to do strange things!

For example, shortly after Dave and I had our misunderstanding, I tried like crazy to preach like a Billy Graham or a Charles Spurgeon! Talk about trying to be dynamic! Wow! I raised more devils than I could ever possibly cast out.

A particular preservice prayer meeting that I attended about this time stands out in my mind. I can still almost hear myself praying. It seems as if I had temporarily forgotten that God wasn't hard of hearing

It certainly doesn't take a psychologist to see through what had happened to me. I was like the frightened teenager walking through a cemetery whistling in the dark. From a biblical viewpoint I was reminded of the prophets of Baal when they confronted Elijah in the "who is the real Jehovah" contest (1 Kings 18:28-29).

"They cried aloud, and cut themselves after their manner with knives and lancets, till the blood gushed out upon them. . . . there was neither voice, nor any to answer, nor any that regarded."

Certainly I was not addressing my prayers to some strange God; I had simply lost that sense of quiet confidence that comes when one lives close to God. "Thou wilt keep him in perfect peace, whose mind is stayed on thee because he trusteth in thee" (Isa. 26:3).

The end result was that I began working in the energy of the flesh instead of in the power of the spirit. It now seems strange to me, but I never recognized this until after I was revived! The moment God filled my heart with his Holy Spirit, he opened the scriptures to me that made this an undeniable fact. Scriptures like the following became more meaningful than ever before.

"I am crucified with Christ: nevertheless I live, yet not I, but Christ liveth *in me* . . ." (Gal. 2:20). "For we are *his* workmanship . . ." (Eph. 2:10b). "But ye are not in the flesh, but in the Spirit, if so be that the Spirit of God *dwell* in you" (Rom. 8:9).

For the Holy Spirit to be able to minister through one's life he must relinquish himself to the Spirit's control. To be filled with the Spirit implies that one is controlled and empowered by the Holy Spirit. All too often we equate some unusual emotional feeling with the infilling rather than control. For some, the Holy Spirit will "calm them down," while for others he will "fire them up," but in either case the emotions will be controlled and empowered.

During the days of the revival, when God seemed nearer than life itself, I personally noticed a drastic change in my emotional expressions. By nature I have always been an outgoing person and quite "emotional." I can cry about as quickly as a distressed woman. I am excitable. I love to laugh and joke. Whatever I do I put my whole being into it.

With the fresh newness of life came new control over my emotions. Two weeks after the revival began I became suddenly aware that I had not entered into any light frivolous conversations. I noticed an attitude of seriousness and solemnity toward life that gave greater depth to my Christian experience. I simply, literally, "quieted down" as my emotions were brought under new management. As I "live in the flow," the Spirit continues to keep my every emotion under his control. I can also tell when I get "out of the flow." Invariably when self asserts itself, cries out, and wants to be taken off the cross, I revert back to the same light, frivolous attitudes that seem to hinder my optimum effectiveness.

The expression of "tiptoeing in the presence of God" seemed to express the attitude of those who experienced revival. (See Ecclesiastes 5:2.) One evening Dr. Ross Minkler and I were praying together at the parsonage when I used that expression. Later when he was flying back to California, he began thinking about it and penned a chorus that became a favorite for the remainder of the revival. (See page 66.)

This is the reason many persons were surprised that a meeting could be so intense in its feelings and yet have a subdued, relaxed atmosphere. One should not be surprised at this, however, for the Holy Spirit always brings order and sense into every situation (Gen. 1:2, Acts 2:11).

Even those who were very naturally emotional in their

Used by permission of Ross Minkler

verbal expressions of rendering praise to God were made aware that this can sometimes be "of the flesh" instead of "in the spirit." Most of us were hesitant in using such expressions as "Praise the Lord" or "Hallelujah" lest attention be focused on self rather than on Jesus (John 3:30). I'm not suggesting that all verbal expressions do this, but there is danger if it becomes a habit. Of this I am positive—many people feel they have to "work-up" the spirit, and they do so by loud emotional expressions. This, is *not* of the Spirit, and one should avoid it. Of course there is the spontaneous joy and exuberance that often demand expression. This will never be out of order or focus attention on self or be something that is worked up or stimulated. It will be of the Lord, in his way, and in his time. One should never be afraid or skeptical of these periods of rejoicing. We need them (Acts 13:52).

To have self under the Spirit's control is an absolute necessity if we are going to be used effectively of God. In some cases, such as Doris, it may be our tempers, while in others it may be the natural human desires. One man said to me during the revival, "You know, Brother Tarr, there was a certain young woman that I always wanted to answer the phone when I called a particular place of business. I was never unfaithful to my wife, but I had a desire to talk with this young woman as I felt a certain attraction for her." When he was filled with the Spirit he was cleansed of this subtle, secret sin!

In a day when many seem to be forever seeking "signs" or some emotional or physical manifestation to assure them they are filled with the Holy Spirit, it seems extremely important that we get this wider perspective of what it means to be controlled and empowered by the Holy Spirit.

It is far better to base one's experience on faith (Acts 15:9, 1 John 5:14-15) than on some emotional experience. If you base it on faith, the Holy Spirit will control such feelings as discouragement, anxiety, fear, and worry.

He will grant control of our tongue in tense situations, and he will continually cleanse our attitudes and empower us to do his will.

Are you walking softly in God's presence?

THINKING THINGS THROUGH

Let's Talk about It

1. What practical effects does revival have on the home-life? List a few.

2. What are the abiding results of the Spirit-filled life?

3. Does the Holy Spirit change our emotional makeup? If so, how? Does the idea of "empowered and controlled" give added perspective to the Spirit-filled life for you?

Your Personal Quest

1. If you have been struggling in knowing that you are filled with the Holy Spirit, read the following scriptures in sequence: Ephesians 5:18; Luke 11:13; Acts 2:38-39; 5:32; Romans 12:1; 1 John 5:14-15.

2. Now ask God to fill you. Take him at his word. Rest your case on the Word of God—not emotion.

3. Then expect God to use you. He will!

8

"Say It Again, Brother Tarr, Say It Again!"

"And David danced before the Lord."—2 Samuel 6:14

It is not entirely a matter of conjecture as to just what the believers did during their ten-day vigil after the ascension of Jesus. Several facts are known, such as: they spent much time in prayer and supplication (Acts 1:14); the group consisted of men and women (Acts 1:14); there were approximately 120 present (Acts 1:15); they were there in obedience to the Lord's previous command (Luke 24:49, Acts 1:4); and they remained in one place and were in one accord (Acts 2:1).

One day while studying some of the references concerning the outpouring of the Holy Spirit, I noticed something that had escaped me before. In 1 Corinthians 15:3-6 we read,

"For I delivered unto you first of all that which I also received, how that Christ died for our sins according to the scriptures; and that he was buried, and that he rose again the third day according to the scriptures: and that he was seen of Cephas, then of the twelve: After that, he was seen of about five hundred brethren at once; of whom the greater part remain unto this present, but some are fallen asleep."

The question arose, where were the other 380 on the day of Pentecost? It is obvious that Christ appeared to at least 500 at one time, yet only 120 tarried in Jerusalem for the promise of the Father.

I certainly don't want to read something into the Scriptures that isn't there, and it is altogether possible and highly probable that those whom God *intended* to be present at Pentecost *were* present! However, it does pose an interesting question, doesn't it? Whatever the case, it is true that 380 of those to whom Christ appeared were *not* present when the Holy Ghost fell. If one should place this in a modern context, I could pretty well hear what the 380 would be saying:

"I just don't have time to stay in Jerusalem for ten whole days!"

"I'm expecting some guests, so you had better get someone to take my place."

"I have an important business engagement that I just can't break. Sorry."

"I can't be away from my family that long!"

"I can't stay but I'll be happy to sponsor someone."

These unknown 380 missed the most spectacular moment in history—Pentecost! By the tone of First Corinthians 15 one can be fairly sure that they came to experience the Holy Spirit somewhere down the line, but they missed that great event that marked the birth of the New Testament church and changed the course of human history.

It was highly significant that they were in *one* place for an *extended* period of time. All too often revival eludes us simply because we do not have the opportunity to spend enough time with fellow Christians. Even as a log will not burn in a fireplace alone, neither can the individual Christian sustain his spiritual fervor in isolation. It appears vital in God's scheme for revival and evangelism that Christians *be together!* Jesus never sent his disciples out alone. They always went in teams (Mark 6:7), and the same is true of the traveling evangelists of the Acts (Acts 8:14; 11:25-26; 16:39-40). There is power in association.

In the fall of 1971, I saw the value of a group of men praying and fellowshiping with each other for an extended period of time. Annually, the Board of Evangelism of the State of Ohio sponsors a week-long institute of specialized training for various state pastors. The 1971 meeting was conducted at a beautiful Lutheran Bible Camp in Fulton, Ohio, in late fall. Elmer Rich, State Coordinator for Ohio, asked Harold Phillips, Adam Miller, and me to serve as guest leaders for this conference. It turned out to be one of the highlights of my Christian experience.

The meeting began on Monday with the showing of a tape-slide presentation of the Anderson revival. One could sense the hunger of these men to experience a new touch from God. Later that same day, I shared my own personal testimony with them and, after explaining the meaning of the word *confession,* asked that they take forty-five minutes to get alone with God and allow him to speak to them. It was a moving experience just to watch these men as they walked out into the beautiful forest to get alone with their Maker. When they returned very little was said about what had transpired in their private confrontation with God, but it was quite evident that God was speaking to each of us.

By Tuesday evening the men were really getting "on fire." We had such a tremendous evening worship hour that the coordinator came to me and said, "Brother Tarr, I'm afraid that we have 'topped-out' a little early. What are we going to do tomorrow night?"

Little by little one could see these men being rekindled with the fire of the Spirit. Once in a while one would say, "You know God spoke to me out on that stump on Monday, and something's happening to me."

One day I noticed a fine young man take another stroll out into the woods alone, and I felt pretty sure that he had something to talk over with God. Later that same day, he stood before the men and related how the fountain of tears had simply dried up within him. "Once," he said, "my heart was tender, and I would often weep for the lost. But for the past few years I have lost this concern, and nothing seems to touch me. But today, the tears returned!" As he spoke the tears were streaming down his cheeks.

For four days, we bathed in the presence of God. God was in our midst in an unusual way, and our conversation centered on him. We went to sleep thinking about God and arose the next day singing his praises.

Each evening we had our corporate worship hour, and I have never heard such singing as came from that small group of thirty ministers. Most of the songs were the old favorites, but I don't recall ever quite hearing them sung like this. There was something about this meeting that dissolved all barriers that would have normally hindered our fellowship. Many in this group of ministers had been denied advanced education, but after a few services, one could sense that we were simply "brothers" in the Lord—there were no big "yous" or little "Is." "We were one in the Spirit; we were one in the Lord."

This was our hour to rejoice! (1 Thessalonians 5:16). Here we were miles away from the nearest town, no inhibitions, no formalities, no fears. Everyone just "let his hair down" and worshiped God like he wanted to. One of our ministers got happy one night when he was singing and he bobbed up and down, up and down, as he sang. I had never seen anything like that, and it reminded me a little of when David brought the ark of God back to Zion, "leaping and dancing before the Lord" (2 Sam. 6:16b).

The camp manager sensed this moving of the Spirit on the camp. He began asking questions and requested the men to sing for him and the cooks after the evening meal on Thursday. Soon after the men left the dining hall, this man sought out one of the ministers and asked him what it was these men had that he didn't have. The minister asked him if he had ever had a personal relationship with Christ. He responded by saying that he had once studied for the ministry, but as far as having a personal relationship with Christ, he wasn't sure. This minister had the privilege of leading him into the experience of salvation. He was born again!

Later that same evening (the last evening we would be together), some of the pastors got together and planned a communion service. Some of us thought it would be quite difficult to plan such a meeting since we had no communion trays, and other items. But the men would not be deterred. They assured us that they would take care of everything.

That evening, Thursday, was without doubt one of the highest moments of my Christian experience. The ministers had planned a nice program, but soon after the service started, they had to disband their plans. God had again moved in on the scene and taken over. (It reminded me of an invocational prayer that a pastor prayed. "O God, please do something that isn't in the bulletin!") Adam Miller read the scriptures concerning the Lord's supper (1 Corinthians 11) and feet washing (John 13).

The men passed the chalice—an ordinary green coffee mug—and one following another we took the bread and drank the cup. This was an interracial meeting attended by eight black ministers and twenty-two white ministers. I was sitting next to an outstanding young black pastor from Cincinnati, Vernon Lambe. He and I broke holy bread together. Then one of the men started singing a hymn, and from that point on, nothing else was said; just singing, crying, rejoicing.

Next came the time for the footwashing. I looked across the room and there sat the camp manager—the Lutheran —washing the feet of a Church of God preacher. He enjoyed it so much (Jesus said we would be happy if we would do it!) that he didn't stop after washing one person's feet. He washed the feet of two preachers! He said that he was making up for lost time.

Finally, the basin was set in front of me. I had never had the opportunity of washing the feet of one of my black brothers. Although I had experienced new love for all my brothers nearly a year prior to this moment, I had not had the opportunity of giving this type of expression to it.

While sitting next to Vernon waiting to wash feet, I couldn't keep from noticing that he had about the longest feet I ever saw—about size 13 I'd say, and my size 7 seemed dwarfed by contrast. I couldn't keep from thinking that if those who had prejudice in their hearts would just wash feet, this might also wash away the prejudice. There just isn't much difference in people's feet. Did you ever notice that? I suppose no one can brag about having

beautiful feet, especially preachers! Except for the difference in size, I saw nothing different in Vernon's feet and
mine. The truth of the matter was that Vernon was the size
I always wanted to be! About 6′2″ compared to my 5′8″.

When I knelt in front of Vernon, I looked up at him and
said, "Vernon, I want to thank you for this opportunity of
washing your feet." I meant it from the depths of my heart.
He looked at me and all of a sudden said, "Hold it, everybody, hold it!" Everyone ceased his singing for a few moments. Vernon pointed his finger at me and said, "Did you
hear what that man said. Say it again, Brother Tarr, say
it again!"

Something happened to me as I washed this man's feet!
When I put his size 13 in the basin and washed his feet I
felt the Holy Spirit surge *through* me *to* Vernon. Unless
you've experienced this, you may doubt the veracity of that
statement, but it is true!

In a few moments it became Vernon's turn to wash my
feet. Someone had taken the wash basin, so he grabbed a
small bucket that was being used to put water in the basins,
knelt on one knee, and putting my foot in the bucket, he
lifted his hand up toward heaven and said, "Glory to
God," and began washing my feet. He told me, "Brother
Tarr, when I put that little white foot of yours in that
bucket and washed your feet, I could just feel God smiling
down on us."

Indeed God must have been smiling down on us. We
were having the time of our lives. Here were two men, one
black and one white embracing each other and singing,
"Makes me love everybody." Here was the short little
preacher, bobbing up and down as he sang the songs. Here
was a man like Adam Miller, standing straight and erect
with a loving smile on his face, reminding me so much of

a pillar. Here was Harold Phillips singing, shaking hands, and embracing these men who knew that he was "for real."

This was revival; revival that came as we, like the disciples, tarried and prayed and interceded unto God till the fire fell. This was love that transcended race and culture, love that transcended the intellectual barriers, love that changed the lives and attitudes of thirty preachers—plus one Lutheran camp manager.

My purpose in sharing this incident is more than simply to relate a high moment in the life of a group of ministers. Rather it is to highlight the fact that we Christians need to spend more time together in prayer, fasting, and fellowshiping. For some, this will be the *only* way revival will ever come. Secondly, we need to recapture the joy of the Lord in our experience. It was only natural that when the one unsaved person on the premise saw the love and joy of the Lord being manifested that he wanted it. This is evangelism at its best. He was drawn to the Lord by the contagious spirit and attitude of these men whose hearts were burning with the love of God.

This might say something about how some of our public services ought to be. Can the unsaved, unbelieving world sense that we are joyful Christians? Is there freedom for expression, freedom to rejoice, freedom to sing, freedom to share, freedom to "be God's happy family"?

It might also say something about the quality of our love and the need of having our hearts cleansed of prejudice and pride. It might say that there will never be a revival of any consequence until the race issue is resolved and we again love as Jesus loved!

THINKING THINGS THROUGH

Let's Talk about It

1. What are some practical ways Christians could spend more time together?

2. Could it be that so many of us are so busy *doing* church work, that we are losing the joy in *being* a Christian? Illustrate.

3. Can any authentic fellowship ever be exclusive in spirit? What are some of the implications true revival has on racism and bigotry?

Your Personal Quest

1. Seek to broaden the circle of your fellowship and concern. Why not make that first move in building a friendship today?

2. Ask God to help you enjoy people more and things less.

9

But What If That Hippie Does Get Saved?

"He eateth and drinketh with sinners."—Mark 2:16

This was one baptismal service that I would not soon forget! Just after praying with the candidates who were going to be baptized that evening, one young man said, "Brother Tarr, when you baptize me, will you hold me under the water just as long as you possibly can?"

A few moments later I lifted my hand and said, "Mike, upon your profession of faith in Jesus Christ as your personal Savior and Lord, I now baptize you in the name of the Father, and of the Son and of the Holy Ghost." Never had I baptized anyone quite like Mike. He had folded his arms across his chest, was smiling slightly, and had the look of heaven on his face. His whole appearance reminded me of the mental image I had formed of Jesus.

The story of Mike's conversion was closely connected with the renewal of a minister in Anderson, John K. Summers, who is one of the finest men I have ever met. Here is his story:

"Looking back upon the past few years in which I have known Jesus Christ is indeed rewarding. From the moment I first came into contact with the Good News my life has been changed. Just two years ago however, something definite and new happened in my life as I came in contact with the moving of the Holy Spirit in what came to be known as the 'Revival of Love' here in Anderson. A fantastic change came about in my life and especially in relation to those about me. For the first time, real divine love began to flow in and through my life. For the first time I was enabled to love people, not just those who would be like I wanted them to be; not just those who looked like I wanted them to look, or those who acted as I wanted them to act, but a love that flowed out to other persons regardless of what they were, how they looked, or how they acted, and continued to love them whether they ever changed or not.

"For the first time I began to see Jesus Christ in everything. Everywhere I turned I saw him and heard him coming through. I could look into the eyes of a long-haired boy and see Jesus and love him. I interpreted television commercials in the light of renewal. "What the world wants to know," and "I've got the spirit" are prime examples. Identification stickers and buttons for Jesus no longer were offensive and it became easy to witness and react to anyone. Prayer took on a new dimension and there came a deep hunger and thirst after righteousness. . . .

"For the first time in my life, love began to flow to my unsaved father who came back to God as a result, and broken relationships were healed completely. The scripture in Proverbs 16:3 became personal as I realized that 'when a man's ways please the Lord, he makes even his enemies to be at peace with him.'

"During the second week of the nightly meetings here in Anderson, God gave me a chance to prove my mettle before him as he called on me to do a very difficult thing.

"The meetings had grown so much that it was decided to conduct them on Sunday afternoons in the various school gymnasiums. There was great excitement about such a meeting and it was to be held at the Southside Junior High School Gym. God was working in such a magnificent way. It seemed such a ripe opportunity to see the unsaved brought to Christ. The Lord had already helped me bring in some who had found real victory, and now a new opportunity presented itself.

"I began to think of a young man twenty-four years of age who had grown up in our Sunday school, and, although he had limited Christian influence in the home, had turned his back upon God. Michael had come home from Vietnam a year before and had now fallen into many open sins. I had seen Mike through many stormy times over the years. His first marriage had been a disaster, and, after a second try, he had given it up completely. He began drinking and in general lived a life of wretchedness. I can remember standing in the emergency room at St. John's Hospital with him after he had been involved in a terrible auto accident. Only by chance and miracle was death averted at that time.

"Later on Mike organized his own rock band and became very adept in the field of rock music. He had long hair and attired himself in what I had looked upon as weird clothing. He was clean and loving, yet a sinner. That day, while I was alone in my study, God spoke to me almost audibly and said, 'Why don't you call Mike and ask him to attend the Sunday afternoon meeting with you.' For a moment it shocked me that such a thought

81

should come to me. Tears began to come into my eyes as I pondered the lost condition of this young man. Swiftly these thoughts pounded in my brain: I had shut him out of my life. I had not really shown him that I cared anymore. I hadn't really loved as Jesus would. I had been critical of his hair, his band, his philosophy, but had never shared Christ's love with him.

"I reached for the phone that day to invite him to attend the mass rally with me. Just as I placed my finger on the dial, God spoke again to me, 'What if he says he will go? You know the attitude of people toward long-haired boys. You might be criticized. Are you willing to be seen with him? What if he asks you to ride with him, would you be ashamed? You had better make sure you mean it before you invite him.' I knelt there in front of the phone that day. With my cheeks wet with tears I prayed and told God that I did not care how he was dressed or what embarrassment might happen as a result. I wanted to see Mike saved and that was all that was important. I rose from my knees once again to dial the number when I was once again interrupted by the same voice. 'What if he should go? What if he should get saved? What if he should not change his outward appearance, and what if he should return to church and witness to salvation? You know how many people in the church would feel about that. What if he wanted to sing in your choir? What if you were faced with open criticism by some in the church? You'd better make sure you mean business because this is going to cost you something.'

"Once again I knelt in front of the phone, this time openly broken and weeping almost uncontrollably. I told God I didn't care what the price of trying to win this soul was. I told the Lord I'd be proud to have him in the church and in the choir, and that I didn't expect him to cut his hair or change his type of apparel. I just wanted his heart right with God.

"That time when I arose from my knees, I began to twist the numbers on the dial. My heart was beating wildly as it began to ring. His mother answered the call. Mike was asleep, but she would convey the message to him and I should call back later. She thanked me for my interest and concern and told me she was almost sure Mike would want to go and that he would appreciate my love and sincerity.

"Later on I returned the call on schedule, my heart in high gear and my blood pressure out of sight. The voice on the other end was that of my prospect, 'Man, I'm getting my hair dry ready to go. When do you want me to pick you up.' Arrangements were completed quickly. We would leave at 2:00 P.M.

"I can never tell you how I felt from that moment on. My heart sang praise within me. I was like a six-year-old leaving the circus. Happiness raced up and down through my body as I made melody in my heart before the Lord. I shall never forget when I climbed into that red sports car with my captive prospect for God. Mike had always demonstrated much love for me, but that day it overflowed. He laid his hand over on my leg and patted me. . . .'John K. I want to thank you for inviting me today. I've been looking for answers. Some of them I have found and some of them I haven't found. Maybe today I'll find the rest of them.'

"Like a tape recorder at double speed, I spieled off to him the news of the great revival that had come to the church. I told him how God had changed my own life and given me love. I asked his forgiveness for not having loved and cared enough for him and others like him. I related quickly the miraculous moving of the Holy Spirit night in and night out. It seemed as if I was in another world in those moments.

"The next thing I knew we were searching for a parking place at the gym and then on our road into that blessed sanctuary where nearly fifteen hundred people had already gathered. Seats were at a premium, but we were directed to the bleachers at the side. Near the third row from the top at the center of the side section there were just two seats. I can never forget making our way across the gym in full view of three thousand staring eyes—the long, red-haired, bearded, strangely-attired twenty-four-year-old youth with a forty-six-year-old suited, statuesque preacher, striding together into a religious meeting that was second to none. I was completely oblivious to what was going on and as I look back upon it, I remember feeling like a king on a throne with a prince at my side, one whom I dearly loved and would have willingly laid my life down for in that hour. I prayed; oh, how I prayed!

"As we seated ourselves, Mike once again laid his hand over on me and took my hand and squeezed it as if to say 'Thanks.' I squeezed about 20 'Glory's' and 57 'Hallelu-jahs' and a thousand 'Thank You Jesus' back. Various testimonies were given; the audience lifted their voices in songs like 'To God Be the Glory' and 'There's a Sweet, Sweet Spirit in This Place.'

"The Holy Spirit began moving in a very wonderful way. Again God spoke to me: I was wearing a little card which said, 'Smile God Loves You.' The voice said, 'Take that card off and pin it on Mike. Tell him that God loves him and that you love him, and that you would like to have a part in helping him to know that love was real in his heart.' O how I struggled over this! It was such a foolish idea, and such a far-out thing to do. Over and over the inner compulsion to do this came. Like a wave it would hit me and then again and again it would continue to come; 'Give him the little card and tell him God loves him and that you love him also.' I became reckless in that moment and with hands shaking and my heart trembling I did it!

"Barbara Creager was singing the verse of 'There's Room at the Cross for You,' and then an invitation chorus. There was a moment of serenity and silence and Mike gripped my hand and said, 'Let's go!' Up we both came and made our way down through the maze of people and out across the gym floor through hundreds of people to the altar where we knelt before an omnipotent, loving, and kind God who didn't care about hair or clothing, only the heart. I was overcome with emotion. I didn't think I could relate to Mike's need in that hour and didn't know what to do.

"As I struggled I realized someone else had dropped to his knees in front of Mike. As I looked up I saw that a young man, Dave Perry, from Asbury was there. 'Let me pray with him,' Dave said, 'I can relate to him, for I've lived this life just like he has.' I inched back a bit and then another young man dropped to his knees with my prospect. It was Mike's cousin. These two young men had been very close but had been separated because of Mike's wicked life and his hair and outward appearance. I listened to the praying and the confession. My prospect was searching for God in open confession of his sin. Tears were streaming from his eyes and it was difficult to see his face as the long hair stuck to the front of his cheeks.

"Dave was giving him instructions and loving him. Stan, the cousin, was openly weeping and intermittently praying

85

for forgiveness also. Then in a moment, Stan threw his arms around Mike's neck and asked him to forgive him for not caring enough and for having shut him out of his life because of his hair and attire. It was a beautiful moment for everyone concerned. I can remember my prospect looking up amid tears and hair and friends and openly confessing Jesus Christ as Savior.

"The afternoon sun had found its way through one of the small windows and a halo of light was resting on the head of the new convert. It was an exhilerating moment of beginning again. I felt I had been born anew myself. Mike shared his witness before the entire audience that day and told the story of finding his way back to God. It was impressive and authentic in every detail.

"Mike was a changed individual from that moment on, and I began to share with those with whom I had never before shared—the spiritually poor, halt, maimed, and blind. God has used his love within to win many. I found I could communicate and that barriers were only man-made. In Christ, there was no generation gap, nor was there any reason for me to avoid a person because of race, color, appearance, or anything else. The Lord took me through an entirely new schooling. I had been trusting too much in outward appearance and not looking upon the heart as God did. I had been afraid of the opinions of others and had sought the approval of men too much.

"O yes, I became known as a hippie lover and even some spoke of our church as 'that hippie church.' You see, young people found a common communication in our worship and they began to come. Mike brought as many as fifteen at one time himself. Youth began to pour into the services. Adults began to stare in unbelief, but God's blessing was indelibly put upon it and today I can testify that scores of them have come to Christ and are living new lives in Christ Jesus. And it all began with a preacher who had never learned to love people, not for what they could mean, not if they would be what I wanted them to be, but love them as they are even if they never changed. Love never changes. It is the one thing that will never fail."

THINKING THINGS THROUGH

Let's Talk about It

1. *Evangelism* has often been associated with the winning of those who are *like* us, while *missions* has been associated with ministering to those *unlike* us. What is the fallacy of this?

2. How can we better handle the cultural gap so evident in our church and society? Are we called on to love or to judge?

3. Can any "fragmented evangelism" be authentic?

Your Personal Quest

1. Converse with someone who seems different from you— even a hippie type. Try to hear what he says to you.

2. Some young men and women in your community have left the church and are now a part of the sub-culture or drug-culture. Let them know that you love them. If you don't, who will?

10

"Praise the Lord, Dad!"

"And the seventy returned again with joy."—Luke 10:17

"Well, we had a great time witnessing tonight but honestly, when we first went out we were scared to death. We were assigned to visit one of the bars in our city, and frankly we didn't know just which one we ought to go to. Neither of us had been in one since we got saved, so it was a pretty shaky experience for us. While we were walking down the street we began praying that God would lead us into the right bar!

"The bar maid laughed when we ordered Cokes, but it wasn't long until each of us had the opportunity to share the gospel with two men who sat next to us. It was wonderful to watch God open the door of opportunity for us to witness. It was a great experience."

One could sense the excitement in the voices of these two Seminarians as they shared with the other members of the Evangelism class. Some of the other students had gone to shopping centers while the rest of the class had visited in homes.

But some will say, "Witness in a bar? I thought the Bible told us to abstain from the very appearance of evil, and here two supposedly Christians are going into a den of sin." That's right, but the scripture also admonishes us to "go into all the world," and we need to remember that severe criticism was leveled at Jesus because he "ate and drank with sinners" (Mark 2:16). If Jesus visited your town, where do you suppose he would go? Could it be that he, too, might walk into one of the bars to tell lonely men of God's love for them? I think so.

It is a sobering fact that those who most need the gospel seldom ever go to church. How then are we ever going to reach them with the claims of Christ if we refuse to go to "where they are"?

One of the most unusual conversions of the revival centered around a Christian man who witnessed in a local bar. It seems that Mary had made careful plans to commit suicide on Sunday afternoon—just three days away. She had purchased a revolver and called her mother-in-law to see if she would take care of her two small children for a couple of hours on Sunday afternoon, between the hours of 3:00 P.M. and 5:00 P.M. At that time Mary planned to go to her hotel room, lock the door, put the revolver to her head, and pull the trigger. Everything was ready and she was determined to go through with it.

Mary had had an unfortunate marriage and soon after their second child came she and her husband were divorced. The man to whom she was now married was in the military service and she was terribly lonely and depressed. She felt that she had nothing to live for, as life had lost its meaning and purpose. Just six months prior to this crisis moment, Mary turned to alcohol and quickly became its victim. She sought for employment but the only job she could find was serving as a bar maid at the Anderson Hotel. Things had gone from bad to worse and there seemed to be no way out.

While serving drinks to several customers on Saturday afternoon—just 24 hours before the appointed hour—a mysterious thing happened. A man stepped up to the bar and, when she started to take his order, he commented that he did not come in for a drink. "I have been led of the Lord to come in here to tell you that God loves you, and that you shouldn't go through with what you are planning. He has happiness for you if you will only trust him." With that he wheeled around and walked out of the bar.

Mary couldn't believe what she had heard! She had told no one of her plans; yet here was a man whom she had never met before who walked up to her and told her that she should not carry out her plans. She asked to be relieved from her post of duty and, after going to her room, she began weeping uncontrollably. "How could that man have possibly known of my plans? Surely God must have told him because there was no other way he could have known about them."

Mary didn't take another drink for the rest of the day. Instead, she called one of her friends and asked if she could go to church with her the next day.

When the song of invitation was sung the following morning during the worship hour, Mary was one of the first to go forward. As I began counseling with her, she told me what had happened. She had the instrument of death in her purse, but was kneeling before the Author of *Life!* As Mary opened her heart to Christ she came to know and experience God's love. She had found peace.

Mary moved from Anderson shortly after she was saved, but I am sure she will never forget that moment when God sent someone to her in her hour of dark despair. A life was spared, a soul saved, and two little children still had a mother because someone was living close enough to God to follow an impulse to witness in an unlikely place, at an inopportune time, to an obviously hardened person. To date we still have no idea who the witness was; we can only thank God for him.

Sometimes we get the impression that before one can win souls he must have years of study and preparation. Some feel that the effective evangelist must memorize scores of "proof texts" so he will have pat answers to every situation. Although I *strongly* believe in a practical, consistent method of training believers in how to witness, we must remember that "the letter killeth, but the spirit giveth life" (2 Cor. 3:6b). One of the vital elements in soul winning is being sensitive to the leadership of the Holy Spirit and to human need. Albert C. Outler, professor of historical theology at Southern Methodist University and also an authority on John Wesley, made the comment that if Wesley had died before he was thirty-seven years old, he would not have rated a footnote in the history books. He added, "The crucial aspect in Wesley's transformation came when his dominant emotion was converted from *passion* to *compassion*. He was always intense and full of feelings and emotion and passion. But it was not until he became compassionate that he became an effective fruitful evangelist."[1]

Personally, I feel that this is the reason revival is so essential to evangelism. Many of us have a passion to

---

[1]From an address delivered at the Congress of Evangelism of the United Methodist Church in New Orleans, 1971.

build great churches and win many people, but all too often the driving motive is ego-centered. Paul said, "For the love of Christ constraineth us" (2 Cor. 5:14a). If we allow Christ to love through us we will be effective, fruitful witnesses also.

The tragedy that often accompanies some of our evangelism training programs is that by the time the evangelist learns the skill, he has lost the zeal! It looks like this:

It should look like this:

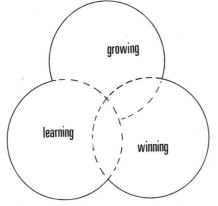

If one waits until he learns enough and grows enough before he evangelizes, chances are *he will never win one single soul to Christ!*

Learning, growing, and evangelizing are interconnected and success comes only as we keep them connected. This is one of the dilemmas facing us today. For years laymen have been listening, supposedly learning and growing, yet still they do not feel competent enough to witness. When will we *feel* adequately prepared to witness? After three years of classroom work—four years—or will it be five? Dare to begin where you are with what you have and you will learn and grow as you evangelize!

It is said that the New Testament church grew more through the burning witness of her informal missionaries than at any other time in church history. When I read the Book of Acts, the excitement almost takes my breath! Acts 9:31 reveals the church in one of her "normal moments":

"Meanwhile, the church had peace throughout Judea, Galilee and Samaria, and grew in strength and numbers. The believers learned how to walk in the fear of the Lord and in the comfort of the Holy Spirit" (LNT).

The element of missions in the Anderson revival gave impetus to personal spiritual growth. Many of those who went on witness teams grew more in one weekend experience than they had in years. Because of my heavy schedule with the church in Anderson, I had but one opportunity of going on a team.

I'll never forget the prayer concern that was evidenced on the part of the twelve persons as they gathered together for a preservice prayer meeting. Each member of the team knew that he would soon be standing before three hundred persons sharing his faith. Half of the group had been converted for only a short time, and this was the first witness team that any of them had been on.

One of the men read the following scriptures to the group before they went into the service:

"When I came to you, brethren, I did not come proclaiming to you the testimony of God in lofty words or wisdom. For I decided to know nothing among you except Jesus Christ and him crucified. And I was with you in weakness and in much fear and trembling; and my speech and my message were not in plausible words of wisdom, but in demonstration of the Spirit and power, that your faith might not rest in the wisdom of men but in the power of God" (1 Cor. 2:1-6).

As pastor of this team, I felt a deep sense of pride and joy as I saw them being used of God mightily in that service. One of the team members, in reflecting on the situation, said, "I became more aware of how God works, and for the first time realized the burden my pastor must bear before each service. I came away knowing that if I carried that kind of burden for my own congregation there would be great victories for Christ. Another benefit in going on the team was that I also found it easier to talk about spiritual matters on a person-to-person basis after I returned home!"

My two older daughters who were then 17 and 13 also went on several witnessing teams, and it was very gratifying to watch them grow as they witnessed for Christ.

For years we have had a standing rule at our house that when a young man takes one of our daughters out on a date, he must have her back at the agreed hour. Not ten minutes, not five minutes, not even one minute after the prescribed hour! Our eldest daughter, Barbara, didn't like the rule too well (neither did Jim who is now her husband) and I am sure that Beverly, Bethany, and Bobi won't like it any better when they get to the dating age, but it is a rule that is "undiscussable."

There were times, of course, when Barb and Bev were

95

out on church or school activities that lasted longer than we could anticipate, and as most parents would do, when they came in after I had retired for the night, I would usually go growling to the door, fumbling with the lock, and after getting the door open would ask, "Where in the world have you been?"

When Barbara left with a number of other persons to go to Minnesota on a witness team, we had no idea when she would return. The doorbell rang at 4:00 A.M. on Monday morning. Again I went staggering to the door, and when I opened it, my beautiful seventeen-year-old daughter greeted me with a big smile and said, "Praise the Lord, dad! We had a great time." Now tell me, how can anyone fuss when greeted like that?

THINKING THINGS THROUGH

Let's Talk about It

1. How can we as a congregation get out into the world with the message of salvation? How can we evangelize our city?

2. How can we keep our evangelism program from depending too much on what happens inside the church building?

3. Discuss the interrelationship of learning, growing, and evangelizing. What does this say about your own personal growth?

Your Personal Quest

1. Make an effort to get involved in one of the many evangelism training institutes offered by various churches and groups across the United States and Canada.

2. The Lay Witness Mission programs offer excellent opportunities for the laity to get involved in evangelism. Check with your pastor about both of these possibilities.

11

"Sir, Would You Like Me to Pray for You Now?"

"They . . . expounded unto him (Apollos) the way of God more accurately."—Aquila and Priscilla, Acts 19:26

I knew something had happened when he came up and put his arm around me and asked for forgiveness. It seems that he had spoken sharply to me at a minister's meeting a year or so before, but I had forgotten the whole affair. At any rate, I assured him that I forgave him and thanked him for sharing with me because I knew what it meant to him.

What had happened was that Reverend Samuel Lovelace had just experienced "Instantaneous Revival!" It is a mistake to think that renewal comes in the same manner and in the same way to everyone. I had my own experience that spanned several months, but here on one sunny August afternoon a minister of the gospel was transformed within a few moments.

Of course, God works differently with various persons, which is part of the wonder and excitement of being a

Christian. Few parents deal the same with every child. They take into consideration each child's disposition, reactions, and personality. So it is with God. He sometimes seems to delight in surprising us with new methods of bringing joy and happiness back into our lives. It's a good thing, too, for all of us have the tendency of mistaking the method for the spirit. Just because God chooses to work in one manner at one time does not restrict him from working in another way at other times. The limitations are placed by us—not God.

Several persons in Anderson discounted the revival simply because there was no "formal preaching." Had we had the traditional two songs, prayer, one song, offering, special song, and a three-point sermon, they would have considered it a bonafide revival—regardless of whether anything happened or not.

It should be said to those who are fearful that a strong lay movement threatens both the minister and "preaching" that they have nothing to fear! "It pleased God by the foolishness of preaching to save them that believe" (1 Cor. 1:21b). Authentic revival and evangelism always has been and will continue to be dependent on the *kerygma* ("proclamation of the gospel"). It is regrettable that some ministers were skeptical of the strong lay involvement which characterized the entire 1970 revival movement across the United States. In reality, such lay-oriented movements buttress the position and accentuate the need for solid, biblical-centered preaching. Those ministers who experienced revival will testify that preaching has never been more exciting or fruitful than it is now.

But back to the story. Sam is now one of my dearest friends. He has always reminded me of a lawyer in his approach to the task of preaching. He is extremely regi-

mented, nonemotional (some would say he is dry),
scholarly, and an excellent pastor and preacher. I could
never remember seeing him shed a tear; that is, until that
afternoon in the park. What was it that so completely
revolutionized his life in a matter of moments? Rather
than my telling it, let him share for himself:

"It was August 24, 1971. I was sixty-nine years old and
had served twenty-three of my fifty-one years in the pas-
toral ministry in one congregation. Like most ministers,
my life centered around the usual routines of pastoring
a local congregation. There were teaching responsibilities,
administrative duties, building-fund campaigns, the reloca-
tion of a congregation into a new community, the erecting
of a new building, and the care and oversight of the pastorate.

"Now at the beginning of my sunset years, I sensed a
consciousness of an inner and growing hunger for a
deeper, more meaningful life. In fact, it had become more
than a hunger; it became a quest. Through those inter-
vening years, I had sought out opportunities for learning
and fellowship experiences at retreats, camps, study
groups, prayer cells, and the like—all of which contributed
to the development of both a deeper experience and a
greater hunger.

"For some sixteen years I had attended an annual
Minister's Week conference sponsored by the Anderson
College School of Theology. This was a week devoted to
study, fellowship, and sharing. The 1971 Minister's Week
was on the theme 'The Evangelistic Task of the Church'
and Reverend Charles Tarr and Reverend Dale Whalen
were the guest leaders.

"Monday evening Reverend Tarr informed us that we
were going to share in a witness experience with a youth

99

group the following day. This youth group was a part of the 'Jesus Generation' which was just then appearing on the horizon in the Anderson area. This group was going from town to town and from door to door with a simple testimony of God's love.

"The thirty-two ministers who were in attendance all felt rather reluctant in going on such an expedition, but in good faith we agreed to accompany them. We met in a city park in Alexandria, Indiana, and shared lunch with the youth group. Then we sat in a large circle for a time of worship. One could 'feel' the gap that separated these two groups. Half the circle was youth—some with rather long hair and garbed in their traditional blue jeans and sweat shirts. The other half was made up of 'dignified clergymen.' One of the young men began playing his guitar and led the group in singing. Although the barrier seemed to lift a little, everyone was still quite 'up tight' about the whole affair. It was obvious that both groups were afraid of each other, but I sensed more fear in us clergymen than in the youth! We wondered what this group of youth was going to get us into!

"It was then that Reverend Tarr asked the group to break up into teams, one youth with each minister. A young woman, perhaps in her early twenties, with long and flowing hair, dressed in blue jeans, with a heavy chain about her neck supporting a metal cross, came up and announced that I was to go out witnessing with her that afternoon! We formed another circle to pray, and this time one could feel the generation and cultural gap being spanned by the love of God.

"We were assigned certain streets to visit in Alexandria, and we were to go from house to house with a simple word of witness. Our transportation from the park to our assigned area was an old Cadillac hearse—a veritable fugitive from the junkyard, now resurrected and pressed into service. However, nothing about it had been changed. It was still black and somber, decorated with the melancholy scrollwork common to vehicles of its vintage and character. There was no mistaking its original purpose; but, needless to say, the deportment of the present occupants bore no resemblance to the solemnity and dignity characteristic of those formerly transported by it.

"Arriving at our assigned territory, we proceeded down the streets, going from house to house with a very simple message. The young woman would knock on the door and say, 'Hi! We're just a couple of Christians who stopped by today to tell you that God loves you and has a wonderful plan for your life. And, we love you too!' She then gave the person a bookmark bearing the sign of the fish, the *ichthus,* and explained, 'We would like to give you this bookmark to put in your favorite book. The sign (pointing to the Greek letters of the ichthus) simply means, "Jesus Christ, God's Son, Savior." The early Christians had to use this sign because they couldn't share their faith as we are today. We hope that every time you look at this marker, you will remember that a couple of Christians came by one day just to tell you that God really does love you.' At this point she would give them her best smile and close by saying, 'Have a good day!' That's all she said. She wasn't selling or asking; she was sharing God's love.

"I learned that this young lady had been converted only four and a half months before from the drug culture. Although she had been involved in the many sins associated with that culture, she was now radiantly telling of God's love and her love for people. She was doing it with exuberance and sincerity. I learned that in ten days this group of some thirty youth had called at more than ten thousand homes! In fifty years of ministry, half a century, I had never made that many calls. I was challenged by it and even more *convicted* by it. Here was the answer for my search for meaningfulness in Christian service.

"It was a very humbled preacher who came back to the city park. As we were leaving, I thanked the young woman for the privilege of learning from her that day. As I turned to go something within impelled me to say to her, 'When you pray, will you pray for me? I have a spiritual need.' Being somewhat blinded by tears, I again turned to go only to feel the tug of a little hand on my sleeve and hear a voice saying, 'Sir, would you like me to pray for you *now?*' She motioned for some of the other youth to come and, within a few moments, I was surrounded by these precious young people interceding with God on my behalf. One big, rough-looking, bearded fellow laid his arm across my shoulder and together we prayed. I remember one young man saying, 'Bless him, Lord, bless him!'

"There were no words capable of describing what happened that day at the Alexandria city park! In a very real and new way I experienced a spiritual renewal in such measure and intensity that rendered me unable even to talk about it for the next two days. Even now, almost a year later, as I write these lines there is reassurance unspeakable and full of glory!

"Naturally such an experience has to be shared, but for two days I could do nothing but weep as I tried to relate it to several of my colleagues. Then on Thursday morning, God presented the opportunity. Marvin Hartman led in our morning devotions, and after he concluded, a holy silence fell upon us. Everyone seemed afraid to move and no one proceeded to make the usual announcements.

Reverend Tarr broke the silence by looking directly at me, saying, 'Sam, now is the time for you to share with us.'

"As best I could I related the incident that had happened in the park when the young people prayed with me. I could hardly speak for the tears, but I managed to relate how that somewhere down the long ministerial trek, I had lost the vibrance, the thrill, the wonder, and the exuberance of the Spirit-filled life. As far as I knew I had been faithful in preaching the Word of God and in shepherding the flock assigned to me by the Lord. But the fire was burning low in my soul. I needed a fresh touch from God, and when that little girl tugged at my sleeve and said, 'Sir, would you like me to pray for you now,' I either had to refuse or accept. I accepted. As these youngsters prayed for me, the Holy Spirit so filled my heart that I could hardly contain it. For two days I have been trying to share it with you, but couldn't for the tears. But, gentlemen, I'm a new man. Something has happened within. I feel God's love burning within me. In closing I would just like to say, Hi! I'm just a Christian that dropped by today to tell you that God loves you and has a marvelous plan for your life. I love you too! Have a good day!"

After giving this tremendous testimony, Sam sat down and then God moved in again. Another minster rose quietly and confessed a deep need. Immediately upon sharing this need, those nearest him surrounded him and laid their hands upon him and prayed. One after another, ministers, young and old, shared different problems and concerns. One young man asked a middle-aged minister for forgiveness in holding a bad attitude toward him; another confessed to having been short-circuited by feelings of inferiority and fear. For nearly two hours these men confessed to each other, prayed with one another, were reconciled to each other, and enjoyed a measure of the same renewal that Sam experienced in the Park!

Some might wonder if the experience lasted in Sam's life. Again, let him speak for himself. "Now almost a year has passed and the renewal has not diminished; rather it has increased. From the beginning I established two disciplines for myself: First, sometime, somewhere, each day I would wait in God's presence for a reaffirmation of spiritual guidance. Second, at least once each day I would share God's love with one other person. There are good days—days of spiritual growth, days of deepening faith, days of harvest, and the end is not in sight!

"I share this with you to verify the fact that spiritual renewal is possible. God is doing a new thing in this generation, and the gentle breeze of the Holy Spirit is blowing once more over his church. This is revival in *our* time. It is a revival of love." Thousands of persons will experience revival *only* as they begin to evangelize. The lepers were cleansed as they went their way in obedience to Christ's command (Luke 17:14). He also says we are to go . . . teach . . . baptize! (Matt. 28:19-20).

THINKING THINGS THROUGH

Let's Talk about It

1. How can one guard against becoming a professional Christian? How can we recapture the exuberance of the faith?

2. In what practical way could we share in an experience such as is related in this chapter? How might we do this in our community?

Your Personal Quest

1. The next time someone expresses a spiritual need to you, pray for him then. He needs help and quickly.

2. Watch for an opportunity to tell someone that God loves him and that you love him, too. Just watch God work.

12

I Guess I Just Missed It!

"Nothing is more odious to wisdom than too great cleverness."—Seneca

Annually the Coral Ridge Presbyterian Church in Fort Lauderdale, Florida, under the direction of Dr. James Kennedy, sponsors a clinic on personal evangelism. In February of 1971, I attended this clinic. During one of the evening sessions one of the trainers, Mrs. Joan Walters, made a statement that I felt was quite profound and caused me to think more deeply.

Joan was serving as my trainer for the clinic. One evening we were standing in the narthex of the church when a gentleman in his middle fifties began explaining to me how God can bring success out of an apparent failure when one witnesses for Christ. Early in his training he attempted to present the gospel to a young man, but the best he could do was to read the plan of salvation to him. He could go no further. He was quite sure that he had miserably failed God. He went home discouraged and ashamed.

However, he was to learn a lesson that each of us must learn. That is that God is the Lord of the harvest and he alone can make his word bear fruit. This young man accepted Christ after he had gone home and contemplated on what he had heard. In pointing this young man out to me he said (in his exact words) "He in turn has won several, several, many, many persons to the Lord!"

The three of us were still standing in the narthex and I asked them another question, "Does this happen often around here?" Actually I was referring to the mood of excitement and enthusiasm that was impossible to overlook in this church as people shared with each other about the particular experience they had had that evening in witnessing. Joan, however, thought I was referring to John's comment about his reading the gospel to the young man. She quickly retorted, "Are you serious? Really? Listen, if we just read the gospel we would be in serious trouble. We have to *know* the gospel!"

There it is! This statement highlights a truth that is so simple and so obvious that we run the perilous risk of overlooking it. We are in trouble if we do not know the gospel. To Joan this meant that she had to know the Word of God well enough to intelligently communicate it to those whom she visited. She worked diligently in the memorization of scriptures and illustrations. Even more important, I sensed that she had coupled this knowledge with a sincere love for those around her who did not know Christ. I had the privilege of being with her when she introduced a young twenty-three-year-old college student to Jesus Christ. She not only read the scriptures; she knew them!

When I asked Joan how she became so skillful in handling the Word of God, she commented that she had been in a program of personal evangelism training for more than five years. She had first been a trainee and, after a long period of specialized training, she was now training others how to witness effectively.

The manner in which she had been trained was the key to her success. While many are constantly searching for more tools and methods to assist them in the training of the laity for the task of evangelism, it appears to me that they are not the heart of New Testament evangelism. The strategy we employ is more important than the tools or methods of evangelism we develop.

It is important to remember that strategy and methods, strategy and tools, and strategy and plans are not synonymous terms. Whenever anyone talks about learning a certain "plan of salvation," he does not intend that to mean that it is the *only* way to present the claims of Christ upon the souls of men.

There are always new and better ways of doing things, and any "tool" that one might develop is only a tool that might meet a need at a certain time in the life of the church. It may be less effective at other times. We would not want to be so naive as to feel that any method or tool would meet the needs of our church on an indefinite basis.

One of our most difficult tasks at this point is to un-learn a concept that has hamstrung the church for many centuries. For too long we have placed the main respon-sibility for evangelism on the professional ministry. Dr. James Kennedy comments that 99 percent of God's army is A.W.O.L.[1] The laity has been deceived into believing that it is the work of the pastor to win souls—not theirs!

Amazingly, a tiny mistranslation in our Bibles may have

[1]*Evangelism Explosion,* James F. Kennedy, (Wheaton, Illinois: Tyndale House Publishers, 1970), p. 5.

contributed to our misunderstanding at this point. We have been operating on "the fallacy of the misplaced comma" in the fourth chapter of Ephesians! In this famous passage Paul is describing the various gifts and offices which the risen Christ has given to the church. Most of the older versions and some of the newer ones translate Ephesians 4:11-12 in this sense:

"And his gifts were that some should be apostles, some prophets, some evangelists, some pastors and teachers, for the equipment of the saints, for the work of the ministry, for building up the body of Christ."

The apparent meaning of this is that the evangelist or pastor has a three-fold task:

1) To equip the saints;
2) To do the work of ministry, and
3) To build up the body of Christ.

Actually there should be no comma between these first two phrases.[2]

Even a different preposition is used. The Greek says *pros, eis, eis* which would be better rendered "for," "unto," "unto." A more literal translation then would be that Christ has given pastors and teachers to the church "for the equipping of the saints unto the work of ministry, unto the upbuilding of the body of Christ."

Phillips correctly paraphrases, "His gifts were made that Christians might be properly equipped for their service." Thus the pastor is to be the enabler, the trainer of his laymen to do the work of ministry.

Evangelism in depth came up with this proposition:

---

[2]*The Christian Persuader,* Leighton Ford (Harper & Row, N.Y., 1966), p. 48.

"The growth of any movement is in direct proportion to its ability to mobilize its entire membership for continuous evangelistic action."

Yet, the perplexing question that keeps arising is how does one mobilize the entire church for evangelism? More than once sincere pastors have attended evangelism conferences and became highly motivated only to go back to their parishes terribly frustrated and disillusioned because the "plan" didn't work successfully in their congregation.

Regretfully, some men have alienated and confused their laymen, rather than equipping and training them. Far too many ministers have motivated their people to evangelize, only to see this excitement dissipate because they told the people what they ought to do instead of showing them how it could be done!

God's strategy for world evangelism was revealed in Jesus Christ. Around this strategy Jesus oriented his entire ministry. This is why the scriptural accounts of Jesus contribute our best and only inerrant *Textbook of Evangelism.* At first glance it might appear that Jesus had no plan, but this is one of the marvels of his strategy. It is so unassuming and silent that it is unnoticed by the hurried churchman.[3]

We have dubbed this strategy as the "inverted funnel concept." Jesus began with a few (only twelve disciples and there is abundant evidence that even among the twelve he spent a great deal of extra time and effort with Peter, James, and John) and depended on these men to carry out his strategy of world conquest. He lived with them, worked with them, ate with them, and taught them for nearly three

---

[3]*The Master Plan of Evangelism,* Robert E. Coleman, (New Jersey: Fleming H. Revell Co.) pp. 18, 19.

years. It was a highly effective means of imparting eternal truths. They were, in the best sense of the word, his disciples (students). Jesus did not begin with the multitudes, nor did he depend on them to carry out his strategy. To diagram it, it would look something like this:

| Calling of the the twelve | Jesus lived with His disciples and imparted His truth to them |

How vastly different this is from most of our "crash programs" of evangelism. "Monday evening we are having a special visitation program to reach our community for Christ. Everyone come to help us in this tremendous exciting effort." What happens? On the first night we have a respectable number. The people go out and invite their friends to church (we called this "discover and invite" during the 50s), but within a few weeks the enthusiasm dies out, the number dwindles, and six months later everyone has forgotten the whole idea. In its wake comes added frustration to the pastor and the whole church. We started out on the wrong end of the funnel!

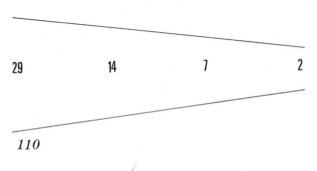

29   14   7   2

One of the chief objectives in personal evangelism training is to provide the pastor and a few laymen the opportunity to recapture this basic strategy of Jesus. In any such attempt we have some mammoth obstacles to overcome:

1. Our life-styles are so different from those of Jesus' day that it is extremely difficult (if not totally impossible) for a pastor to live with his laymen as Jesus did with his disciples. We live in a transient, busy, time-demanding, and changing society.

2. Because of tradition the pastor is called upon to give so much of his time to other important matters that he feels he cannot devote a large block of his time to a few members of his church. Consequently, even after a long pastorate, many of us have not been successful in training even a few skilled witnesses.

3. We are all a little reluctant to carefully reexamine our priorities. Hence we are often giving our optimum efforts to good endeavors; but minimal efforts to the *main priorities* of ministry.

Granted this process seems painfully slow; it must have seemed so with the disciples too! No doubt they would have loved for Jesus to have sent large envoys of evangelists to Rome, Ephesus, Corinth, and other major population centers in hopes of converting that heathen empire within two years! Ironically, Jesus never traveled more than fifty miles from the place of his birth, and even after his resurrection he admonished the disciples to *wait* until the Holy Ghost came upon them. Then, he said, the conquest would begin!

Joan Walters is just one of many thousands across the United States who feel that it is not enough to simply read the gospel to those who are unsaved. We must know the gospel, depend on the Holy Spirit to prepare the hearts of those to whom we witness, and then actually go into the harvest fields while they are white unto harvest.

I remember reading a story by Edgar Allen Poe, "The Purloined Letter," which highlights one of man's dilemmas in his quest for truth. Here a group of detectives, who were extremely skilled in their search for concealed evidence, was charged with the task of recovering a stolen letter that was being used as blackmail against an important political figure. The Chief of Detectives, the Prefect, took the greatest care to see that the culprit's residence was searched so thoroughly that it would surely be found. In his words:

"I took the building, room by room. . . . We examined first, the furniture of each apartment. We opened every possible drawer; and I presume you know that, to be a properly trained police agent, such a thing as a secret drawer is impossible. . . . The fiftieth part of a line could not escape us. After the cabinets we took the chairs. The cushions we probed with the finest long needles you have seen me employ. . . ."

On and on he went with the search, but to no avail. Where was the letter? On a trumpery filigree cardrack of pasteboard, that hung dangling by a dirty blue ribbon, from a little brass knob just beneath the middle of the mantlepiece! The meticulous Prefect had outwitted himself by overlooking the obvious.

God help us that we may not overlook the simple strategy employed by our Lord in evangelizing the world.

THINKING THINGS THROUGH

Let's Talk about It

1. Discuss the "inverted funnel concept" of evangelism training. What is your opinion of this strategy?

2. What is the basic difference in the "Discover and Invite" concept and actually confronting someone with the claims of Christ on his life.

3. Is inviting people to church, helping them with their problems and such, evangelism or pre-evangelism?

4. React to the statement that "evangelism is incomplete until we stand at the heart's door of the sinner and confront him with the claims of Christ."

Your Personal Quest

1. Begin immediately to learn the basic truths necessary in leading someone to Christ.

2. Make yourself available if your pastor asks you to join him in an evangelism training program.

13

A New Wind Blowing!

"The wind bloweth where it listeth and thou hearest the sound thereof . . ."—Jesus, John 3:8

Not long ago a young man sang a song that touched a responsive note deep within me. I remember only one line: "In my darkest night I saw a light, and it was *Jesus!"*

Revival always comes during dark times. The seventeenth century Protestant Reformation and the Wesleyan Revival of the eighteenth century are prime examples. Almost everyone is aware of the deteriorated condition of the church preceding the Protestant Reformation. In church history it is known as "the dark ages."

Across the channel from England in the eighteenth century France was being torn apart by the seeds of discontent. This finally erupted in one of the bloodiest revolutions recorded in European history. The very names of Danton, Robespierre, Guillotine, and Napoleon bring a sense of fear to one's heart.

England averted this catastrophe mainly by the preaching of one man—John Wesley. Thousands of changed lives changed a nation and resulted in sweeping social reform, such as the first child labor laws, women's voting rights, and the first labor union.

The United States has been going through a very dark time in her history as a nation, especially during the decade of the 60s. Who will forget such incidents as the shooting of James Meredith in 1962, or the date of November 22 when we heard the tragic news "John F. Kennedy is Dead!" The memory of Watts in 1965 and Detroit in 1967 and Memphis in 1968 with the assassination of Martin Luther King, Jr., still haunts us. Our nation was shocked to a state of unbelief as we witnessed these incidents on television. We prayed for respite and yet the darkness continued to move in upon us. Robert Kennedy joined his brother in death in the fall of 1968 as another assassin's bullet found its mark. College campuses were the scenes of unrest and violence. On May 4, 1969, it culminated in the death of four students at Kent University. The whole nation was wearied and disillusioned with the bloodshed of thousands of lives in an undeclared war that we seemed to be unable to win and too proud to lose. During the 60s *a nation wept for her dead!*

No wonder one scholar commented: "We came down to the end of the 60s frustrated, tired, discouraged, and disillusioned. The decade of the sixties had been a violent one and we wondered, What's going to happen in the seventies?"

It was also during this decade that theologians pronounced the death of God and gave the church the dubious status of being "His tombstone." Church attendance waned and many were ready to throw in the towel, feeling that Christianity was all washed up. John Lennon on one occasion was reported to have said that his group of singers, the Beatles, was more popular than Jesus Christ!

Perhaps even more tragic was that the church seemed to be unaware of the tremendous social, racial, economic, and religious revolution that was taking place in our country. One leader incisively said, "The tragedy of the sixties was that the church ignored a revolution."

Then God stepped into the picture! The Anderson Revival was only one very small segment of a much larger and widespread movement of the Holy Spirit. Most of us would have said what happened in Anderson was just an unusually good "revival" had it been confined to this one city. But when one rises above one locale, and gets a wider perspective, he is suddenly aware that a new wind is blowing across America. Nineteen seventy marks the birth of the Jesus People Movement, and even though many were disturbed with some of its excesses, it appears that these young people are playing for "keeps." Revival was the number one religious news story in 1971!

Even as I write this concluding chapter, I am reading of a continued revival in Canada, and South America has been a ripe harvest field for more than half a decade! No one can or will say who was responsible for the spiritual phenomenon of revivalism, but perhaps Fanny Crosby said it best, "To God be the glory, great things he hath done!" One college coed exclaimed, "It's all His, It's all His!"

I sensed it over two years ago, and I have learned that revival is much like the wind. Although one cannot control the wind, contain it, harness it, adequately explain it, or preserve it, he can dare to stand out in it and let it blow through his hair and sting his eyes until the tears come! God does not ask us to understand these things, but he does expect us to have the courage to stand in the wind that "bloweth where it listeth."

It is difficult for me to understand, but many are ignoring revival. They want to play it safe, take shelter, and isolate themselves from this movement. As the tragedy of the sixties was that the church *ignored* a revolution, even so, the *danger* of the seventies is that she will sleep through a revival!

I hear three sounds in the wind—"thou *hearest* the sound thereof."

The first is the voice of many witnesses eager to share the good news of the gospel of Christ. Themes such as "Fulfilling the Great Commission in this Generation," "Mobilizing the Church," and "We're Gonna Change the World" are becoming household words in the community of believers.

Pins and buttons reading: "Smile, God Loves You!" "My Jesus Lives," "One Way," plus many others are positive indicators that Christians, young and old, are becoming bolder in their witness and more fervent in their love for the Christ whom they serve.

[Meaning: Jesus is first; you are second; I am third.]

I'M
THIRD

Practically every denomination in the United States is sponsoring major conferences on evangelism. Thousands are returning from them with a renewed zeal to accelerate their efforts to move aggressively into all segments of our society with the message of hope and reconciliation. The battle strategy has reversed from the defensive to the offensive.

Christians everywhere are gathering around the priority task of evangelizing the world and, as a result, many of the barriers that once separated true believers are beginning to diminish. The *task* has become the *thing.* During this decade the greatest concerted effort ever put forth by Christendom to evangelize an entire continent will take place.*

Youth are excited about Christ to a degree that is making the staid, unmoving element of the church rather uncomfortable. The very name of Jesus has more "shock" power in it than obscene words do! Youth by the thousands have his name on their lips, no longer in profanity, but in praise. And, now they ask, "Who is John Lennon anyway?"

Dr. Billy Graham recently said, "I'm now fifty-two years of age, but I sincerely believe that the greatest days of my ministry are yet to come." Thousands are being won to Christ through the proclamation of the Word in mass evangelism. I have personally witnessed the conversion of more unsaved persons during the past two years than I did during the other seventeen years of ministry.

We have an effectual door of opportunity in spreading the gospel that is unprecedented. Twenty-five major TV

---

*Key '73 is an effort to Call the North American Continent to Christ in 1973.

market areas reach 95 percent of our nation's population. Radio has staged a comeback—"everywhere you go there's radio."

However, the most obvious indication that a new wind is blowing is in the arena of lay involvement. No longer are laymen contented to let the pastor do all the work of ministry. Many feel that this lay movement is our greatest, if not *only,* hope for world evangelism. Wherever laymen become involved in an authentic program of evangelism, new life comes surging into their lives like a flood.

I sense in laymen a willingness to vulnerability—they have played it safe long enough. Anyone can sit in a church and listen to a sermon, or join in the singing of a hymn, or participate in supporting the church financially, but to win souls—this is a different matter indeed!

For too long we have been fearful that we might make a mistake, say the wrong words, or offend someone! Thank God at last we are taking Christ seriously. The "Lo" is with the "Go" in Matthew 28:19-20.

BUT, I hear another sound in the wind—the footsteps of impending tragedy if we do not respond to the call of God. To be brutally frank, this revival frightens me. Not in the sense that I am fearful to meet the Lord, but fearful for our nation, our church, perhaps even for our world, if we fail to respond. Could it be that God is preparing a people, a remnant who will be willing to "go through the fire" if necessary for our blessed Lord? Few of us would have the courage to do it alone, but as we join hearts and hands together we could be among that number "They came out of great tribulation, and have washed their robes, and made them white in the blood of the lamb" (Rev. 7:14).

Somewhere in the back of my mind, or perhaps in a

small corner of my heart, I keep hearing these faint foot-steps of tragedy. My Christian brother, are you ready to join in with the thousands of others who have preceded us in being true to Christ, regardless of the cost?

Our prayer should be that of Habakkuk: "O Lord, I have heard thy speech, and was afraid: O Lord, revive thy work in the midst of the years, in the midst of the years make known; in wrath remember mercy" (3:2).

Then I hear another sound that makes my heart leap with joy! I hear the distant sound of the trumpet of the Lord. Not long ago I sat in a motel with several leaders of major denominations of the United States. We were dis-cussing the implications of revival when one of the men said, "You know, I don't expect to die!" He was utterly sincere. He feels that Jesus is going to return before he lives out his three score and ten.

I saw a bumper sign on an automobile recently that read, "In case of the rapture, this vehicle will self-de-struct!" Regardless of our varying doctrinal views of eschatology, we know that this world is destined for de-struction.

More songs have been written concerning the second coming of our Lord during the past few years than at any other period in recent history. Our own Bill Gaither has penned one of the greatest, "The King Is Coming."*

> *The market place is empty,*
>   *No more traffic in the streets,*
> *All the builder's tools are silent,*
>   *No more time to harvest wheat;*

---

*© Copyright, 1970, by William J. Gaither. Used by permission.

Busy housewives cease their labors,
  In the courtroom no debate,
Work on earth is all suspended
  As the King comes through the gate.

Happy faces line the hallways,
  Those whose lives have been redeemed,
Broken homes that He has mended,
  Those from prison He has freed;

Little children and the aged
  Hand in hand stand all aglow,
Who were cripples, broken, ruined,
  Clad in garments white as snow.

I can hear the chariots rumble,
  I can see the marching throng,
The flurry of God's trumpets
  Spell the end of sin and wrong;

Regal robes are now unfolding,
  Heaven's grandstands all in place,
Heaven's choir is now assembled
  Start to sing Amazing Grace!

O, the King is coming,
  The King is coming,
I just heard the trumpet sounding
  And now his face I see—
O, the king is coming,
The King is coming,
Praise God, he's coming for me!

Even so, come Lord Jesus! The issue facing us *now* is: Who will answer? We hear the sound, we feel the gentle breeze, we sense the moving of the Holy Spirit, but who will answer? Who will answer? Who?

THINKING THINGS THROUGH

Let's Talk about It

1. Do you feel that our nation may be on the threshold of a great spiritual awakening?

2. Many feel that the Lord's coming is near. Are there indications that might suggest this?

3. What would we as a group be doing differently if we knew the Lord would come next year?

Your Personal Quest

Join in with the thousands of others across our nation who are praying for a worldwide awakening. Do not be weary in prayer. Expect a miracle!

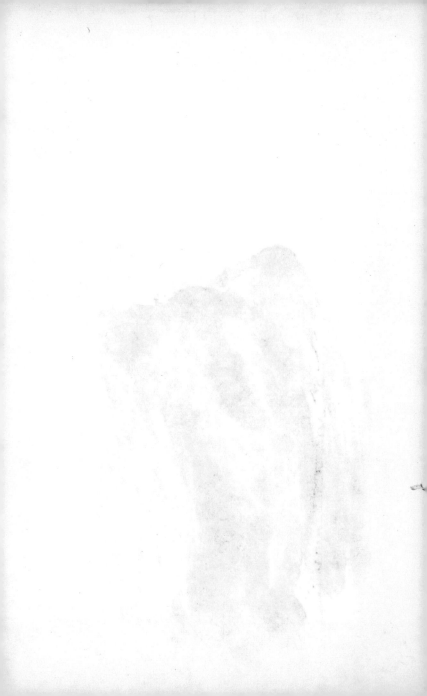

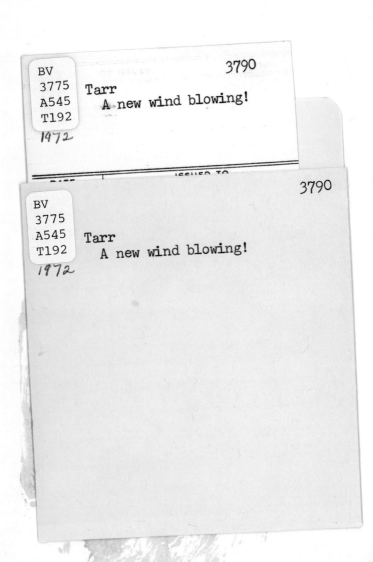

BV
3775
A545
T192
1972

3790

Tarr
    A new wind blowing!